"The clinical training path is quite opaque for aspiring psychologists, and the opportunity for reflecting on aspects of professional development vary considerably between courses, so it is great to see a book to fill that gap. I think this book is relevant to psychology graduates seeking a career in clinical psychology, as well as trainees and recently qualified clinical psychologists. This is a career path in which we continue learning and reflecting on our practice and what we bring to the role throughout our career, and the varied topics covered mean there is something to offer even for those of us who have been in the role a while."

—**Dr Miriam Silver**, *Consultant Clinical Psychologist and Founder/Administrator of www.clinpsy.org.uk, the website for aspiring clinical psychologists*

"This significant and timely publication is sure to become a trusted guide for individuals attempting to make their way along the intricate pathway of professional and ethical practice. Originally conceived as a text for aspiring to newly qualified clinical psychologists, the depth of consideration of the complexities of developing a professional identity while maintaining a critically reflective stance will be of utility to practitioners from an array of professional backgrounds and a range of experience. The book contains deft and frank explorations of issues such as risk, trauma, power and boundaries, how they unfold and the challenges of managing them within an ever-changing social and political context."

—**Dr Anna Daiches**, *Clinical Director, Doctorate in Clinical Psychology programme at Lancaster University*

Professional Issues in Clinical Psychology

Professional Issues in Clinical Psychology: Developing a Professional Identity Through Clinical Psychology Training and Beyond offers insights from a range of trainee, recently qualified and experienced clinical psychologists as they reflect on the process of developing their professional identity through consideration of dilemmas and issues they experienced through clinical psychology training.

Reflecting the breadth of the profession and the range of services in which clinical psychologists work, the chapters highlight the different types of roles that clinical psychologists are expected to undertake throughout training and post-qualification. The book provides practical clinical recommendations that can be applied in work settings in line with contemporary research, policy and guidance, as well as personal reflections from the authors on how managing professional issues has shaped their practice as a developing clinical psychologist.

Developing a professional identity as a clinical psychologist is vital in learning to navigate these challenges. The process by which a professional identity develops is an individual journey. However, *Professional Issues in Clinical Psychology* offers aspiring, trainee or qualified clinical psychologists – and other healthcare professionals – with a contemporary resource around professional issues which might be encountered within clinical psychology practice.

Will Curvis is a clinical psychologist in the NHS, working mainly in acute inpatient physical health and neuropsychology services with people with long-term physical health problems, pain problems or neurological conditions. He also works as a clinical tutor for the Doctorate in Clinical Psychology programme at Lancaster University.

Professional Issues in Clinical Psychology

Developing a Professional Identity Through Clinical Psychology Training and Beyond

Edited by Will Curvis

Routledge
Taylor & Francis Group

LONDON AND NEW YORK

First published 2020
by Routledge
2 Park Square, Milton Park, Abingdon, Oxon OX14 4RN

and by Routledge
52 Vanderbilt Avenue, New York, NY 10017

Routledge is an imprint of the Taylor & Francis Group, an informa business

© 2020 selection and editorial matter, Will Curvis; individual
chapters, the contributors

British Library Cataloguing-in-Publication Data
A catalogue record for this book is available from the British Library

Library of Congress Cataloging-in-Publication Data
A catalog record for this book has been requested

ISBN: 978-1-138-48297-5 (hbk)
ISBN: 978-1-138-48298-2 (pbk)
ISBN: 978-1-351-05626-7 (ebk)

Typeset in Times New Roman
by Apex CoVantage, LLC

Contents

Figures

Contributors

Sophie Allan is a trainee clinical psychologist at the University of East Anglia. Prior to trainee Sophie was an assistant psychologist in an Early Intervention in Psychosis service and head of patient and parent involvement in young people's mental health services. Sophie has a particular interest in service user involvement, co-production and psychosis. https://orcid.org/0000-0002-3601-0580

Helena Coleman is a trainee clinical psychologist at Lancaster University. She has a background in forensic psychology and has a clinical interest in compassion-focused therapy and narrative approaches. https://orcid.org/0000-0002-3318-151x

Anne Cooke is a Consultant Clinical Psychologist. She is Principal Lecturer and Clinical Director of the Doctoral Programme in Clinical Psychology, Salomons Centre for Applied Psychology, Canterbury Christ Church University, UK. https://orcid.org/0000-0003-4241-8280

Laura Cramond is a clinical psychologist who, prior to training, completed a BSc and MSc in Forensic Psychology and gained experience working in clinical and research posts in forensic settings. Since qualifying from the Doctorate in Clinical Psychology at Lancaster University in 2015 she has worked in clinical health psychology services focused on supporting individuals with the emotional impact of living alongside physical health difficulties. She has an interest in third-wave therapies including acceptance and commitment therapy, compassion-focused therapy and mindfulness. https://orcid.org/0000-0002-2924-2690

Will Curvis is a clinical psychologist in the NHS, working mainly in acute inpatient physical health and neuropsychology services with people with long-term physical health problems, pain problems or neurological conditions. He also works as a clinical tutor for the Doctorate in Clinical Psychology programme at Lancaster University, having trained there himself in 2012. Will is involved with the *Beyond the Therapy Room* and *Clinical Psychology Fringe* events (www.psychologyfringe.com), which aim to promote innovative ways to improving psychological wellbeing through service user involvement and community working. Will is also a member of *Sharing Stories* (www.sharingstoriesventure.com), a collaborative aiming to improve knowledge and understanding between mental health professionals and service users in Uganda and the UK. https://orcid.org/0000-0002-2512-7003

Sarah Davidson is a clinical psychologist. Having completed a BSc in Psychology and MSc in Forensic Psychology, she worked in forensic, prison, and substance use services, before commencing clinical training. Since qualifying from the Doctorate in Clinical Psychology at Lancaster University she has worked in a number of NHS settings connected to the Offender Personality Disorder (OPD) Pathway, including an Intensive Intervention and Risk Management Service (IIRMS) for individuals who offend in Merseyside, and a psychologically informed consultation service for Offender Managers in the National Probation Service. She currently works in a specialist forensic psychology service with individuals at risk of offending. https://orcid.org/0000-0002-0468-9170

Nicola Edwards is a clinical psychologist. She works in a secondary care community mental health team in North Wales. She has a special interest in working with people who have experienced complex trauma. https://orcid.org/0000-0003-0475-6916

Liam Gilligan is a clinical psychologist currently employed by Norfolk and Suffolk NHS Foundation Trust. He has a particular interest in the mental health of young people and how to best work with those who present with 'complex' difficulties. He is currently trying to learn to juggle, with embarrassing results. https://orcid.org/0000-0002-5554-3884

Denise Herron is a consultant clinical psychologist currently employed by Norfolk and Suffolk NHS Foundation Trust. She has a particular interest in supporting staff development and wellbeing. https://orcid.org/0000-0002-0841-0739

Hayley Higson qualified as a clinical psychologist from Lancaster University in 2017. She currently works as a senior clinical psychologist in an older people's mental health service in the National Health Service. She has a significant interest in clinical community psychology and is an active member of the *Psychologists for Social Change* network. https://orcid.org/0000-0001-5458-5794

Melanie Hugill is a senior clinical psychologist in a Community Learning Disability Team. She qualified in 2016 from the Lancaster Doctorate in Clinical Psychology after completing the course on a part-time, bespoke pathway. Melanie has extensive pre-training experience working with individuals with learning disabilities in both inpatient and community settings. She is passionate about ensuring the rights of this vulnerable population are heard and upheld. https://orcid.org/0000-0001-9659-5421

Rebecca Hutton is currently working as a senior clinical psychologist in NHS adult acute inpatient and community settings in the West Midlands. She has also practised as a mental health social worker in the North West of England. Rebecca's wide area of interest is adult mental health, in particular working with those who have experienced trauma and have been labelled as having personality difficulties. https://orcid.org/0000-0002-4871-7014

Dr Ailsa Lord is a clinical psychologist who, prior to qualifying from the Doctorate in Clinical Psychology at Lancaster University in 2015, worked in primary care mental health services, forensic mental health and forensic learning disability hospitals, and community learning disability services. Since qualifying she has worked in Later Life Community Mental Health and Memory services in the North-West of England, where she is interested in the use of cognitive analytic therapy with older people, and offers supervision and reflective practice groups to other professions within the team. https://orcid.org/0000-0002-5730-1758

Javier Malda-Castillo is a trainee clinical psychologist at Lancaster University. His research interests include psychotherapy effectiveness, mentalising and attachment processes. Javier has a clinical interest in psychodynamic approaches and has undertaken training in group-analysis and intensive short dynamic psychotherapy (ISTDP). https://orcid.org/0000-0002-6059-2912

Lindsay Prescott is a second-year trainee clinical psychologist studying for the Doctorate in Clinical Psychology at Lancaster University. Lindsay has prior experience working as an assistant psychologist in an adult neuro-rehabilitation service and has also spent a number of years working privately as an assistant psychologist in the medico-legal arena specific to adult neuro-psychological assessment. Lindsay also worked as an assistant psychologist within a community learning disability service before entering doctoral training. https://orcid.org/0000-0003-1186-152X

Masuma Rahim is a clinical psychologist, writer and lecturer. She teaches on the University of Surrey Doctorate in Clinical Psychology and has authored academic papers in the areas of developmental trauma, the management of poor sleep quality and substance use in young people. Clinically, she has interests in the areas of neuropsychology, public health and working with people who identify as lesbian, gay, bisexual and trans. In addition to blogging, she writes about health and current affairs for press publications including *The Guardian*, and regularly appears on television and radio discussing mental health, as well as matters related to multiculturalism and race. https://orcid.org/0000-0002-7880-9737

Bethan Roberts completed her clinical psychology doctorate at Lancaster University. Since qualifying in 2015, Bethan has worked as a clinical psychologist within adult learning disability services in the North West of England and has been involved in the development and evaluation of a human rights–based risk assessment tool which can be used in both learning disability and adult mental health services. https://orcid.org/0000-0003-0101-743X

Thomas Rozwaha is a second-year trainee clinical psychologist studying for the Doctorate in Clinical Psychology at Lancaster University. Thomas completed an MSc in Molecular Neuroscience before entering doctoral training. He saw the importance of clinical psychology in the context of people with neurological difficulties when a family member was diagnosed with Motor Neurone Disease. Since entering doctoral training, he has gained clinical experience of neuropsychological assessment and formulation during his clinical placements. https://orcid.org/0000-0002-3454-1345

Sarah Savekar is a clinical psychologist from Staffordshire. Sarah's background and experience is in working with complex and developmental trauma in adult mental health inpatient services and with looked after children. Sarah works mainly using a cognitive analytic approach, and focuses on attachment and trauma when understanding distress. Sarah draws on cognitive analytic therapy and attachment theory when consulting with staff teams. Sarah's academic interests include neurobiological theories of trauma and child development. https://orcid.org/0000-0003-4825-5099

Graham Simpson-Adkins is a clinical psychologist working at Liverpool Community Learning Disability Team in Mersey Care NHS Trust. He also works in private practice. https://orcid.org/0000-0002-2440-7900

Richard Slinger is a clinical tutor on the Lancaster University Doctorate in Clinical Psychology Programme, and a consultant clinical psychologist specialising in working with children and in supporting school systems around children's mental health. Richard has led the professional issues teaching and assessment strand on the Lancaster programme for a number of years. https://orcid.org/0000-0002-6095-7061

John Timney is a second-year trainee clinical psychologist studying for the Doctorate in Clinical Psychology at Lancaster University. After completing a PhD in Biochemistry and several years working in the pharmaceutical industry, John refocused his career onto clinical psychology, volunteering as an assistant psychologist in a charity organisation and later a brain injury rehabilitation service before entering doctoral training. https://orcid.org/0000-0001-8838-6312

Roisin Turner completed her clinical psychology doctorate training at Lancaster University in 2015. Since qualifying she has worked in adult community mental health teams within the North West of England, and more recently within Lancashire Care NHS Foundation Trust. She uses an integrative approach to therapy, with particular interests in compassion-focused therapy and emotion-focused therapy approaches. https://orcid.org/0000-0003-3894-5002

Helen Walls is a clinical psychologist specialising in child mental health. She has experience of working in mainstream and learning disability-specific child and adolescent mental health services (CAMHS) in the midlands and north west of England. Consultation and individual/family clinical work are the primary focus of her day-to-day work using developmental, attachment, cognitive and systemic psychological models to inform practice. Helen has a particular interest in clinical supervision and this was the focus of her doctoral thesis. https://orcid.org/0000-0001-7043-8298

Preface

This book is something of a labour of love; the initial idea came together from discussions with other people in my cohort while I was training as a clinical psychologist. Many of my conversations with my colleagues on the programme centred around our developing identity as clinical psychologists. We spent a lot of time talking and thinking about how the professional and ethical issues we faced in our practice helped shape our thinking and decision-making, as we began to make sense of what sort of psychologist we wanted to be.

The Doctorate in Clinical Psychology programme at Lancaster University places great emphasis on reflective practice and we were encouraged to think critically about our experiences while we were training; indeed, many of the chapters in this book were developed from assignments written by people during their training about a professional issue they faced in practice.

Since qualifying, I have learned that we often have to make complex professional judgements or decisions where there is no immediate *right* answer. It is vital to be able to do this confidently and competently, within the boundaries of the professional guidance and codes of practice available to us. However, we also must balance this with a critical perspective – considering the individual and unique circumstances of the situation we find ourselves in. We have to think carefully about how we manage the anxiety and uncertainty that this can leave us with.

The process by which a professional identity develops is, of course, an individual journey. However I hope that this text offers aspiring, trainee or qualified clinical psychologists with a starting point for reflecting on professional issues which might be encountered within clinical psychology practice. More broadly, I hope that it is relevant to a range of other professional groups too – indeed, any healthcare professional who works with people may find him/herself facing some of the issues highlighted in this text.

The stories and reflective discussions combined in this book introduce a broad range of relevant professional issues that commonly arise in our work, within the context of research, national policy and clinical practice. Our aim in putting this book together has been to offer insights into the reflective process the authors have taken in developing their professional identity as a clinical psychologist – I hope this is useful in helping you to think about your own.

Will Curvis, Editor

Foreword

Richard Slinger

Professional issues in clinical psychology training

What are professional issues? Is this the same as professional dilemmas or problems? Or is it to do with the question of how to work professionally? Or maybe even what is a professional? What does it mean to be professional or to be a professional?

To some extent, the answers to questions like these depend on your frame of reference and the context in which the professional is working. Does this relate to us just when we are in paid employment, or all the time? Can we ever switch off from being professional? Is it acceptable to act in ways that might be considered 'unprofessional' when we are not at work?

I facilitate the teaching around professional issues with trainees beginning the Doctorate in Clinical Psychology programme at Lancaster University. One exercise we use involves generating a list of behaviours that they consider to be potentially 'unprofessional'. We then plot these on a graph according to whether these things are never acceptable, or whether they might be allowed or even needed in certain circumstances.

Typically, this will lead to a number of things that might be illegal, harmful or clearly outside the remit of our job role in some way. However, this usually leads to a discussion around grey areas and contextual factors that might influence whether a particular behaviour is seen as professional or not.

So we may believe that, for example, losing our temper with someone, or not telling the truth, might be clearly unprofessional. But would it be acceptable to show your unhappiness or even become angry if you saw clear discrimination or poor treatment of another person? Are there times when we have to withhold the truth or certain facts in order to avoid someone (or ourselves) being put at risk? How much would we bend the rules if we had a good rationale that doing so would be in a person's best interests?

So if being professional (or unprofessional) can mean many things, how do we define what being professional is, and how do we learn to be this *thing*?

Being professional is not as simple as reading and following guidelines. Human beings are complex things. The role of a clinical psychologist largely involves working with human beings, and of course we are human beings ourselves. So the potential for complexity and grey areas is vast. There are few hard and fast rules in our field, and the answers to most questions about professional issues and dilemmas tend to start with "Well . . . it depends . . .".

The research in this area suggests that whilst psychologists know what professional guidance asks them to do in response to certain dilemmas, they often consciously and deliberately don't follow it (Goodman, 2000).

"Hard and fast rules alone do not ensure that you can steer through the choppy ethical waters of practice" (Hawkins & Smith, 2006, p. 252).

Many of the professional issues and dilemmas we deal with are also complex because they relate to *wicked problems* (Rittel & Webber, 1973) on a wider societal, political or economic scale. Wicked problems are by their nature impossible to solve because of features such as being too complex to fully understand, too many people and contradictory opinions being involved, the interconnectedness of problems with other problems or the sheer cost of trying to fix them.

For example, on an individual basis, we might have a dilemma about how to respond to an adult client who regularly misses appointments. Do we simply follow a policy that tells us to discharge them? There might be good professional reasons for doing this. But what if we were aware of the influence of other wicked problems such as poverty (cost of transport to appointments), or employment insecurity (taking time off work to attend), or stigma (telling family or employers that they have a mental health appointment), which then relate to our own wicked problems such as economics (NHS efficiency and cost savings)? Would we be minded to bend the rules and give them one more appointment? The influence of wicked problems potentially make these dilemmas much more complex.

"[Professional dilemmas] . . . exist whenever there are 'good' but contradictory reasons to take *conflicting and incompatible* courses of action" (Kitchener, 1984, p. 43).

So how do we learn to navigate the best way to respond to professional issues, difficulties or dilemmas in light of this complexity, and what skills do we need?

The Health and Care Professions Council (HCPC), our professional regulator, defines professionalism as:

> a meta-skill of situational awareness and contextual judgment, allowing individuals to draw on a range of communication, technical and practical skills, and apply the appropriate skills for a given professional scenario. The true skill of professionalism may be not so much in knowing what to do, but when to do it.
>
> (HCPC, 2016)

So while the HCPC set out standards for professional behaviour, they simultaneously define the ability to follow those rules as a much more complex skill.

In our teaching on the Lancaster programme, we outline a model for how we might develop our own stance and values relating to professional issues most effectively.

Internally Constructed Knowledge (what you already know, but might not recognise)	Socially Constructed Knowledge (what you/ we learn together)	Externally Constructed Knowledge (what you need to learn from others)
• Past experience of success and challenge • Intentions (the "why") • Personal values (or what you give value to) • Aspirations	• Professionalism • Shared values Shared commitments • Shared expectations of professional behaviour	• Guidance and policy (e.g., Health and Professions Council, British Psychological Guidance) • Evidence of best practice • Knowledge of NHS context, past and future

Figure 0.1 Internally, socially and externally constructed knowledge

In this model, we propose three types of knowledge that we can bring to bear on dilemmas we may face.

First we have *Externally Constructed Knowledge*, which might be research, professional standards and guidelines. These are the things we cannot know until we are told them or have read them, and are essential in guiding us to the best practice or best response to a difficulty or dilemma. However, how common is it that a standard or guideline can tell us in enough specific detail what to do in a given situation? Policies and guidelines often only give us an outline of what to do, not the specifics.

So what else do we have to draw upon? We have *Internally Constructed Knowledge*, comprised of our personal and professional experience, our values, hopes and our ideas of why we want to do this job in the first place. This is based on our own unique experiences in both personal and professional situations, including success and failure, from which we have learned something about the *right* way to approach things.

While important, this is not enough either, as this is only our own opinion on how things should be done. Argyris (1991) argues that people often rely on four basic values in decision-making: (1) to remain in unilateral control, (2) to maximize winning and minimise losing, (3) to suppress negative feelings and (4) to be as rational as possible.

> People consistently act inconsistently, unaware of the contradiction between their 'espoused theory' and their 'theory-in-use', between the way they think they are acting and the way they really act.
>
> (Argyris, 1991)

So in addition to these, we can use *Socially Constructed Knowledge*, which is what we share and construct for ourselves as a community of people who make up a professional group. These might be shared ideas about what it means to be a clinical psychologist, what we expect from ourselves and others in the same group and what we have seen or heard from other members of the group (both good and not so good) that has taught us something about professionalism.

Learning the competence to deal with professional issues as part of clinical psychology training should involve the development of, and use of, all three types of knowledge. And in this model, being *professional* means acting, responding and behaving in ways that are in line with policy and the evidence base, in line with our personal values, but also in line with what we as a professional group feel is *right*.

Our aim on the Lancaster DClinPsy programme is not to teach people what to do in every possible set of circumstances, or even to see professional skills as something uniquely distinct. In line with the HCPC (2016) definition of professionalism, we feel that ethical decision-making is rarely about making the right decision; it is usually about making the *best* decision in the circumstances in which we find ourselves.

In summary, how might we think about the process of developing a professional identity as a trainee clinical psychologist? Here are some starting points.

- Be aware of research, guidelines and best practice that could be helpful.
- See issues and dilemmas as existing within systems and contexts which are bigger than, and have an influence on, the individuals involved.
- Understand our own values and principles around what it means to be professional.
- Understand our emotional reactions, biases and our 'whys', and put our thinking and reasoning centre stage.
- Use supervision and peer discussion to help formulate our position and response to professional issues and dilemmas.

References

Argyris, C. (1991). Teaching smart people how to learn. *Harvard Business Review*. Retrieved from www.enablinginnovation.co.uk/documents/Argyris-Teaching_Smart_People_How_to_Learn.pdf

Goodman, D. (2000). *Ethical dilemmas in psychological practice: A study of registered psychologists in Queensland* (Unpublished doctoral dissertation). James Cook University, Queensland, Australia.

Hawkins, P., & Smith, N. (2006). *Coaching, mentoring and organizational consultancy: Supervision and development*. Maidenhead, UK: Open University Press.

Health and Care Professions Council. (2016). *Standards of conduct, performance and ethics*. Retrieved from www.hcpc-uk.org/publications/standards/index.asp?id=38

Kitchener, K. S. (1984). Intuition, critical evaluation and ethical principles: The foundation for ethical decisions in counseling psychology. *Counseling Psychologist*, *12*(3), 43–55.

Rittel, H. W. J., & Webber, M. M. (1973). Dilemmas in a general theory of planning. *Policy Sciences*, *4*(2), 155–169. doi:10.1007/BF01405730

Challenges in learning to deliver psychological therapy through clinical psychology training

Chapter 1

Managing and using countertransference emotions within therapy

Roisin Turner

Summary points

- Countertransference can be seen as a way to assist the therapist understand his/her relationship with the client, and despite the value of using countertransference as a therapeutic tool, therapists can feel challenged and stressed by these emotions.
- There are a number of ways in which countertransference emotions can be explored and understood, for example, through supervision, personal therapy and professional support.
- Using psychological theories such as attachment theory and psychological formulation can aid understanding of a client's difficulties and our own responses.

To understand the process of countertransference, it is important to first consider transference and the therapeutic relationship. Essentially, *transference* refers to the client's attitudes and feelings, often towards an early attachment figure, which is displaced onto the therapist (Freud, 1912). *Countertransference* refers to the thoughts, emotions and fantasies experienced by the therapist which have been triggered by the client, but are to do with or arise from the therapist's experiences and reactions (Jacobs, 1999). Countertransference is an unconscious process which the therapist only becomes aware of through careful introspection (Heimann, 1950). When a therapist is making efforts to build a therapeutic alliance, both transference and countertransference responses are likely to occur.

Psychotherapy is itself a human interaction (Norcross & Wampold, 2011), and both transference and countertransference are essential aspects of any relationship (Brenner, 1982). Freud's early work highlighted his beliefs that countertransference within therapy should be recognised, managed and overcome (Freud, 1959). Countertransference in modern psychotherapy is viewed positively and is seen as a way to assist the therapist in understanding his/her relationship with the client, for example, through interpersonal patterns (McDougall, 1978). Countertransference offers a direct source of information about clients, revealing what may be happening within the therapeutic relationship, and therefore what happens in the client's life external to the therapeutic setting (Heimann, 1960). It acts as a guide to learning more about the client's state of mind (Eagle, 2010; Frawley O'Dea & Sarnat, 2001) and provides access to the unconscious feelings and behaviours of the client (Wilson, 2013).

Despite the value of using countertransference as a therapeutic tool, clinicians often feel challenged and stressed by these emotions (Rothschild, 2006; Sherman & Thelen, 1998). Therapists can experience strong reactions (Farber & Heifetz, 1982), which can be emotionally draining (Guy, 1987), increase vulnerability to burnout and decrease clinical competence (Briere, 1992). The client's transference of negative feelings onto his/her therapist can be challenging and can elicit countertransference experiences such as a sense of inadequacy (Freudenberger & Kurtz, 1990).

Within clinical psychology training, alongside attending university and conducting research, trainee clinical psychologists attend clinical placements to further aid understanding and enhance their clinical practice. During my placements I was encouraged to become more aware of my emotions and responses to clients during sessions and to reflect on these. This can particularly be relevant within clinical psychology training; trainees can lack confidence and be more vulnerable to feelings of uncertainty with the various pressures and new experiences that come with training. These feelings, termed as *professional self-doubt* (Nissen-Lie et al., 2017), may continue to be present once qualified. However it is argued that this can enhance therapists' work, because they are conscious of their own limitations and more likely to resolve barriers to therapeutic progress (Macdonald & Mellor-Clark, 2014). Other countertransference reactions may include guilt related to unresolved personal issues, unhelpful projections onto clients, boredom and impatience (Palmer, 1980). Many countertransference responses are appropriate and necessary, and may be used as tools in the therapeutic relationship. However, dealing with them can nonetheless be challenging and stressful.

In preparation for writing this chapter, I spent some time reflecting on my work with clients, both as a trainee and qualified clinical psychologist. I noticed that for some clients I would remember the positive interactions we had, whereas with others there was a sense of frustration and agitation. I also noticed that I have experienced emotions such as sadness and strong compassion for some clients, particularly when thinking about my work with clients who have restricted choice and power, for example, children and older clients with a diagnosis of dementia. Reflecting on my experiences with clients I worked with during training and post-qualification, this chapter will highlight aspects of our work that I found challenging and discuss the approaches I used to manage countertransference responses.

Use of supervision

During my clinical psychology training placement within an adult community mental health team (CMHT), I noticed that when working with particular clients

I would become frustrated when they did not complete out-of-session work. I did not experience this response with all clients, but it was particularly noticeable when working with one man who presented with low mood. I was surprised by the strength of this emotional reaction and felt uncomfortable that I should feel negatively towards someone I was trying to help. We were using a cognitive-analytic therapy (CAT) approach (Ryle & Kerr, 2005), and the relational nature of this framework meant it was particularly important for me to disentangle my own emotional responses from what was happening for the client.

In clinical supervision, which is mandatory for both trainee and qualified clinical psychologists, I discussed my emotional responses using CAT as a framework to help guide my thinking. We identified that perhaps I expect too much from clients; when they feel hopeless and struggle with motivation and consequently struggle to meet my expectations, I can become frustrated. This makes me feel 'stuck', which then becomes a vicious cycle for both the client and myself. We reflected that their feelings of hopelessness may be being transferred onto myself, and I in turn felt despairing and stuck in my work as a result. At the time I did not share these thoughts with my client as I was concerned that he would find this too challenging and critical. However I did at times feel as if I was being drawn into a 'rescuer' role; on reflection, discussing the 'here and now' pulls that I was experiencing may have helped us to explore the past and current relationship patterns that increased his feelings of hopelessness.

Within supervision I have drawn upon Vygotsky's (1978) *zone of proximal development* to help me consider my work with clients. The theory proposes that an individual can make changes and learn for him/herself if provided with the right tools and concepts. At the start of therapy, not every client has the emotional resources or resilience for change at that time (Skovholt, 2001). In supervision, I also learned the importance of stepping back, not being drawn into client's feelings and reflecting on times when this may be happening. I became able to acknowledge that I have passion and drive, and want to instil this in others. However, I also realized that I need to carefully consider how best to motivate others, particularly when they are not emotionally ready for this.

Through these experiences, I became more aware of the high expectations I place on others and myself, both clinically and personally. Now, when working with clients who have difficulties completing out-of-session work, I try to explore their reasons and be curious about how they can overcome any barriers to this. I also consider with them whether they have conflicting motivations about change; for example, do they fear failure which may then reinforce feelings of hopelessness? Will success in therapy then mean that they will need to take responsibility for how their life proceeds, causing them to feel frightened? When thinking about engaging people in out-of-session tasks, I have learned that it is useful to focus on building the therapeutic relationship first. I then suggest a small (and realistic) out-of-session task to try, aiming to build on gradual successes without feeling the need to rush people.

Personal therapy

I experienced some personal therapy during clinical psychology training. During this, I explored whether I became more frustrated with clients who shared similar insecurities or patterns to myself, for example, being overly self-critical. My personal therapist used a CAT approach and this helped me to reflect upon my past relationships and experiences. We explored how I can become stuck in patterns of thinking or behaving that have originated from childhood experiences and relationships.

There are many benefits to personal therapy for therapists, and I valued having this opportunity during training. Rake (2009) found in her qualitative study that therapists identified both personal and professional benefits to engaging in their own therapy. Timms (2010) identified that clinical psychology trainees reported increased self-awareness, understanding and confidence through personal therapy experience. Being self-aware can be challenging and unpleasant as it involves becoming conscious of internal tensions and conflicts, and revealing these may threaten our view of self. However, personal therapy allowed me to consider more deeply the emotional aspects of therapeutic work, alongside exploring these on a more intellectual level in supervision.

Professional support

Through my clinical placements on training and my post-qualification work, I have found that sharing my experiences of countertransference with peers, colleagues, mentors and supervisors has been invaluable. The British Psychological Society (BPS, 2009) advise in their code of ethics and conduct that clinical psychologists should "seek consultation and supervision when indicated, particularly as circumstances begin to challenge their scientific or professional expertise" (p. 16), and should monitor their personal wellbeing, identifying when they may be negatively impacted by their work. I am aware that I have a tendency to be task-focused and aim to get on with things. Although this can be helpful at times, on other occasions I benefit from sharing my challenges.

I have learned that communicating my struggles does not mean others perceive me as being inadequate, as has been my fear. Within my final year of training I participated in a psychodynamic-based peer group, and found this invaluable to provide continued personal development to explore the countertransference emotions I experienced. It gave me space to increase my awareness of and reflect on my own emotions within clinical practice and hear how others can experience similar feelings.

Theories to aid understanding

Developing psychological formulations has helped me identify the challenges clients have faced and how these have impacted on their past and current relationships. It also allows me to understand how a client responds to and regulates his/her own emotions, and puts his/her responses into context. Using an attachment framework (e.g., Hewitt, 2008) can provide explanations for seemingly unpredictable emotions and this has helped me gain confidence when faced with strong emotions from a client. For example, when working with clients who as children did not have their needs not met by caregivers, they may increase attachment behaviours in an attempt to get their needs met, or they may withdraw (Bowlby, 1969). Gaining an understanding of a client's early attachments can aid greater awareness of current behaviours and how we can help them. Individuals with avoidant attachment styles may struggle to verbalise feelings and interact with others, and offering intervention that encourages this may benefit them. These concepts offer a useful starting point for making sense of transference and countertransference responses.

I have also reflected on other methods I can use to become more aware of my countertransference responses. Ryle and Lipshitz (1974) endorsed the use of repertory grids to help identify and understand countertransference amongst work with clients. The therapist lists his/her clients and personality constructs are developed from considering behaviour, formulation, client's transferences during sessions and the therapist's countertransference responses. The ways in which the grid information can be used provides a new lens with which to view relational patterns. This approach can be used over time with a particular client to highlight changes within the relationship, or enable a therapist to reflect upon patterns that may occur between clients.

Self-care and social support

The National Institute of Clinical Excellence guidelines (NICE, 2009) highlight the importance of clinician wellbeing, for both the individual staff member and to ensure the delivery of high-quality care. It is therefore imperative to recognise and address the early signs of compassion fatigue or burnout. Compassion fatigue may occur when the issues clients bring begin to exhaust the therapist's ability to work effectively (Figley, 2002), and burnout is emotional exhaustion due to prolonged, yet unsuccessful striving toward unrealistic expectations which can be internally or externally derived (Maslach, Schaufeli, & Leiter, 2001). These are considerations that I continue to be aware of now that I am qualified, as this is when I am more likely to be involved in longer-term complex clinical work.

Alongside making good use of clinical supervision, I use indirect means of countertransference management such as physical exercise, rest and relaxation and engaging in enjoyable activities within personal relationships with family and friends. It is critical to use self-care before a crisis occurs, as this is usually when it is needed most but often overlooked (Pope & Vasquez, 2005). The importance of self-care is highlighted by research (Brady, Guy, & Norcross, 1995; Jennings & Skovholt, 1999; Mahoney, 1997; Norcross, 2000). This might include consideration of diet, exercise and self-reflection through different mediums including writing (Pennebaker, 1997).

Conclusion

Countertransference responses can offer valuable insights into the workings of a therapeutic relationship, however they can also be difficult to manage. Crucial to the use of these approaches is self-awareness; being aware of one's own responses to clients and then deciding whether the reactions require an action in response. In addition to the various stressors related to being a clinician, therapists often need to manage the various occupational challenges within mental health services (Figley, 2002; Guy, 2000; Norcross, 2000; Skovholt, 2001). Therefore it is important to be aware of stressors and signs of burnout or fatigue, and be willing to nurture oneself (Pines, Aronson, & Kafry, 1981). It is vital to have a range of resources and support systems in place at times of challenge and stress, and for supervision to provide a safe space to discuss difficult emotions and experiences (Wheeler, 2007).

I continue to make use of professional support through supervision, communication with colleagues and peers, personal therapy and social support through personal relationships. I also use more informal approaches such as physical exercise and relaxation. Through my work with clients, I have learned the importance of being aware of and examining aspects of myself such as my beliefs, values, biases and both my strengths and weaknesses. I feel that the therapeutic relationship is a two-way process and learning about our responses to clients enables us to learn more about ourselves.

Suggested further reading

Hughes, J., & Youngson, S. (2009). *Personal development and clinical psychology*. Leicester: BPS Blackwell.
Johnstone, L., & Dallos, R. (2013). *Formulation in psychology and psychotherapy: Making sense of people's problems*. London: Routledge.
Sedgwick, D. (2016). *The wounded healer: Countertransference from a Jungian perspective*. London: Routledge.

References

Bowlby, J. (1969). *Attachment and loss. Vol. 1: Attachment*. New York, NY: Basic.
Brady, J. L., Guy, J. D., & Norcross, J. C. (1995). Managing your own distress: Lessons from psychotherapists healing themselves. In L. VandeCreek, S. Knapp, & T. L. Jackson (Eds.), *Innovations in clinical practice: A source book* (pp. 293–306). Florida: Professional Resource Exchange.
Brenner, C. (1982). *The mind in conflict*. New York, NY: International Universities Press.
Briere, J. N. (1992). *Child abuse trauma: Theory and treatment of the lasting effects*. Newbury Park, CA: Sage.

British Psychological Society. (2009). *Code of ethics and conduct.* Leicester: British Psychological Society.

Eagle, M. (2010). *From classical to contemporary psychoanalysis: A critique and integration.* New York, NY: Routledge.

Farber, B. A., & Heifetz, L. J. (1982). The process and dimensions of burnout in psychotherapists. *Professional Psychology, 13,* 293–301. doi:10.1037/0735-7028.13.2.293.

Figley, C. R. (2002). *Treating compassion fatigue.* New York, NY: Brunner-Rutledge.

Frawley O'Dea, M. G., & Sarnat, J. E. (2001). *The supervisory relationship: A contemporary psychodynamic approach.* New York, NY: Guilford Press.

Freud, S. (1912). The dynamics of transference. *Standard Edition, 12,* 97–108.

Freud, S. (1959). Future prospects of psychoanalytic psychotherapy. In J. Strachey (Ed. and Trans.), *The Standard edition of the complete psychological works of Sigmund Freud* (Vol. 20, pp. 87–172). London: Hogarth Press.

Freudenberger, H. J., & Kurtz, T. (1990). Risks and rewards of independent practice. In E. A. Margenau (Ed.), *The encyclopedic handbook of private practice* (pp. 461–472). New York, NY: Gardner Press.

Guy, J. D. (1987). *The personal life of the psychotherapist.* New York, NY: Wiley.

Guy, J. D. (2000). Holding the environment together: Self-psychology and psychologist care. *Professional Psychology: Research and Practice, 31,* 351–352. doi:10.1037/0735-7028.31.3.351

Heimann, P. (1950). On countertransference. *International Journal of Psychoanalysis, 31,* 81–84. doi:10.1007/978-3-319-28099-8_888-1

Heimann, P. (1960). Counter-transference. *British Journal of Medical Psychology, 33,* 9–15. doi:10.1111/j.2044-8341.1960.tb01219.x

Hewitt, M. (2008). Using psychological formulation as a means of intervention in a psychiatric rehabilitation setting. *International Journal of Psychosocial Rehabilitation, 12,* 8–17.

Jacobs, M. (1999). *Psychodynamic counselling in action.* London: Sage.

Jennings, L., & Skovholt, T. M. (1999). The cognitive, emotional, and relational characteristics of master therapists. *Journal of Counseling Psychology, 46,* 3–11. doi:10.1037/0022-0167.46.1.3

Macdonald, J., & Mellor-Clark, J. (2014). Correcting psychotherapists' blindsidedness: Formal feedback as a means of overcoming the natural limitations of therapists. *Clinical Psychology & Psychotherapy, 22,* 249–257. doi:10.1002/cpp.1887

Mahoney, M. J. (1997). Psychotherapists' personal problems and self-care patterns. *Professional Psychology: Research and Practice, 28,* 14–16. doi:10.1037/0735-7028.28.1.14

Maslach, C., Schaufeli, W. B., & Leiter, M. P. (2001). Job burnout. *Annual Review of Psychology, 52,* 397–422. doi:10.1146/annurev.psych.52.1.397

McDougall, J. (1978). Primitive communication and the use of countertransference: Reflections on early psychic trauma and its transference effects. *Contemporary Psychoanalysis, 14,* 173–209. doi:10.1080/00107530.1978.10745534

National Institute for Health and Clinical Excellence. (2009). *Promoting mental well-being at work.* London: National Institute for Health and Clinical Excellence.

Nissen-Lie, H. A., Rønnestad, M. H., Høglend, P. A., Havik, O. E., Solbakken, O. A., Stiles, T. C., . . . Monsen, J. T. (2017). Love yourself as a person, doubt yourself as a therapist? *Clinical Psychology & Psychotherapy, 24,* 48–60. doi:10.1002/cpp.1977

Norcross, J. C. (2000). Psychotherapist self-care: Practitioner-tested, research-informed strategies. *Professional Psychology: Research and Practice, 31,* 710–713. doi:10.1037/0735-7028.31.6.710

Norcross, J. C., & Wampold, B. E. (2011). Evidence-based therapy relationships: Research conclusions and clinical practices. *Psychotherapy*, *48*, 98–102. doi:10.1037/a0022161

Palmer, J. O. (1980). *A primer of eclectic psychotherapy*. Monterey, CA: Brooks/Cole.

Pennebaker, J. W. (1997). Writing about emotional experiences as a therapeutic process. *Psychological Science*, *8*, 162–166. doi:10.1111/j.1467-9280.1997.tb00403.x

Pines, A., Aronson, E., & Kafry, D. (1981). *Burnout: From tedium to personal growth*. New York, NY: Free Press.

Pope, K. S., & Vasquez, M. J. T. (2005). *How to survive and thrive as a therapist: Information, ideas, and resources for psychologists in practice*. Washington, DC: American Psychological Association.

Rake, C. (2009). Therapy and personal development. In J. Hughes & S. Youngson (Eds.), *Personal development and clinical psychology* (pp. 108–123). Leicester: Blackwell.

Rothschild, B. (2006). *Help for the helper: The psychophysiology of compassion fatigue and vicarious trauma*. New York, NY: W. W. Norton.

Ryle, A., & Kerr, I. (2005). *Introducing cognitive analytic therapy: Principles and practice*. Chichester: Wiley-Blackwell.

Ryle, A., & Lipshitz, S. (1974). Towards an informed countertransference: The possible contribution of repertory grid techniques. *British Journal of Medical Psychology*, *47*, 219–225. doi:10.1111/j.2044-8341.1974.tb02286.x

Sherman, M. D., & Thelen, M. H. (1998). Distress and professional impairment among psychologist in clinical practice. *Professional Psychology: Research and Practice*, *29*, 79–85. doi:10.1037/0735-7028.29.1.79

Skovholt, T. M. (2001). *The resilient practitioner: Burnout prevention and self-care strategies for counselors, therapists, teachers, and health professionals*. Boston, MA: Allyn & Bacon.

Timms, J. (2010). A taste of our own . . . therapy: Trainee's rationales for, and experiences of personal therapy. *Clinical Psychology Forum*, *213*, 34–39.

Vygotsky, L. S. (1978). *Mind in society: The development of higher psychological processes*. Cambridge, MA: Harvard University Press.

Wheeler, S. (2007). What shall we do with the wounded healer? The supervisor's dilemma. *Psychodynamic Practice*, *13*, 245–256. doi:10.1080/14753630701455838

Wilson, M. (2013). Desire and responsibility: The ethics of countertransference experience. *Psychoanalytic Quarterly*, *82*, 435–476. doi:10.1002/j.2167-4086.2013.00036.x

Chapter 2

The power of touch

Considering touch and physical contact within a therapeutic relationship

Melanie Hugill

Summary points

- Guidance regarding use of touch in therapeutic relationships is generic and the available research literature is contradictory.
- Consideration of contextual factors will guide ethical decision-making about use of touch in therapeutic relationships.
- Setting boundaries, transparency and seeking supervision/guidance are key aspects for safe practice in the use of touch in therapeutic relationships.

The issue of touch between therapist and client might not be considered in advance; however once you have been embraced by a client or been moved to reach out to comfort a client in distress, the proverbial can of worms is open. This chapter will outline considerations around the role of touch within a therapeutic relationship with reflections from my area of practice in learning disabilities. This chapter focuses on issues to consider regarding the use of touch in therapeutic relationships.[1] The focus is on "culturally appropriate touch" (Zur, 2007, p. 73): touch meant with genuine intentions, for example a handshake, a pat on the shoulder to reassure or a hug to congratulate, rather than touch that crosses the boundary of what may be considered acceptable. However, the appropriateness of any physical contact between a clinical psychologist and a client is an issue of ongoing debate with little consensus (Gutheil & Brodsky, 2008; Reamer, 2017; Stenzel & Rupert, 2004). The clinical psychologist must manage this ambiguity as he/she considers boundary issues in his/her own practice.

Boundaries and the therapeutic relationship

Gutheil and Brodsky (2008) define a *boundary crossing* as "a departure from the usual norms of therapy, that is, the verbal and physical distances normally maintained in a therapeutic interaction" (p. 19). They propose that a *boundary violation* is distinctly different, being exploitative and having potential to harm the client. However, Bonitz (2008) argued the difference is not always easily discerned, and physical contact considered appropriate by some individuals may be thought of as violations by others.

Professional guidance

Several authors have suggested structured guidance for clinical psychologists to use when they are faced with making such decisions (e.g., Calmes, Piazza, & Laux, 2013; Pope & Keith-Spiegel, 2008). However, much of the available professional guidance for clinical psychologists is generic. For example, the Health and Care Professions Council (HCPC) standards of conduct, performance and ethics (HCPC, 2016) state "You must keep your relationships with service users and carers professional" (p. 5). Furthermore, the British Psychological Society's (BPS) code of ethics and conduct (2009) states that the code "cannot, and does not aim to, provide the answer to every ethical dilemma a psychologist may face" (p. 25). Rather, the psychologist is responsible for maintaining the boundaries of the relationship and using his/her clinical judgement in each case. Professional guidance can be helpful in directing decision-making around use of touch and has helped me reflect on my experiences.

Factors to consider

A landmark article by Gutheil and Gabbard (1993) highlighted how decisions regarding boundary crossings cannot be made without considering a multitude of aspects relevant to the context of the therapy. Such decisions may include an evaluation of the type of physical contact to be used, gender and power issues, an understanding of how the client would perceive touch, the motivation for using physical contact and cultural and individual differences.

Therapeutic orientation

According to Smith (1998), the theoretical orientation of the psychologist often influences whether physical contact with a client is deemed to be appropriate. Stenzel and Rupert (2004) found that psychologists who reported their orientation to be more humanistic in nature were significantly more likely to touch their clients than psychologists who reported their orientation to be psychodynamic. However, in a therapeutic setting, even a handshake may be subject to a number of potential issues. There are schools of thought (such as within more traditional psychoanalytic therapy) that believe even a handshake should not be encouraged or offered by the clinical psychologist (Bonitz, 2008). If physical contact is not supported by the theoretical orientation then Smith (1998) surmises that touch must not be used. However, he goes on to say that if touch is not precluded by the theoretical orientation of the psychologist, then an ethical decision is necessary.

Cultural considerations

The type of touch may influence how appropriate it is in different cultures. For instance, a handshake may be viewed by many as an appropriate greeting or farewell gesture in the United Kingdom. Yet individual and cultural differences compound the decision-making process regarding the appropriateness of physical contact. For example, Clance and Petras (1998) report on the decision-making process for a Latino therapist who states that "the idea of not touching in therapy would have been quite foreign and would undoubtedly be perceived as cold, distant and uncaring" (p. 101). However, further research with diverse ethnic cultures is scarce regarding touch in therapy (Zur & Nordmarken, 2018).

In British culture, physical contact such as a pat on the arm, hand-holding or a hug are all physical contacts generally considered appropriate between family and friends. However, the appropriateness of these within a therapeutic setting is not clear, and the decision whether to engage in physical contact in a therapeutic relationship requires much more conscious deliberation.

Gender and power issues

An important part of the deliberation for clinical psychologists should concern the gender and power issues that can be present in a therapeutic relationship. Research in this area is quite dated; Borys and Pope (1989) found significantly more male therapists than female therapists believed that some boundary crossings were acceptable, tending to cross these boundaries more in their practice. However, a study by Pope, Tabachnick and Keith-Spiegel (1987) found that females were significantly more likely than males to hug a client.

Complicating the consideration of gender issues is the imbalance of power found in the therapeutic relationship. Durana (1998) writes that "sex and status determine the politics of who touches when, where and how . . . and women are touched more than men" (p. 270). The clinical psychologist should be mindful of both gender and power issues when making a clinical judgement on whether physical contact is appropriate or not. This will also interact with cultural considerations. Furthermore, those working with children should be aware of the natural power imbalance that exists between children and adults and take steps not to reinforce this when considering touch within such therapeutic settings (McNeil-Haber, 2004). Specific areas of clinical work may require more thought; for example, when working with survivors of sexual abuse, gender, power and age may be particularly salient factors to consider.

The majority of my experience with touch has been within the field of learning disabilities. This area can be particularly complex when deliberating the use of touch as there is the added ethical issue of capacity to consent. People with learning disabilities can find negotiating different types of relationships difficult and I have experienced more boundary crossings in this field than any other during my training. Reflecting on my experience so far, I note that I have rarely initiated touch within my therapeutic relationships, apart from a few times at the closure of longer-term therapies. The embrace has always been mutual and felt like an acknowledgement of achievement. However, I also note that this has been with female clients and not males. I would consider an embrace with a male client much more carefully, reflecting on his understanding of our therapeutic relationship and whether a hug would confuse the boundaries that we had established.

Client perception

Little research has been conducted into clients' perception of being touched within therapy. That which is available suggests several positive effects for clients, including a sense of being cared about and accepted and an increased willingness for self-disclosure (see Calmes et al., 2013 for a brief summary).

However, related to gender and power issues, research has shown that the recipient of physical contact may construe the gesture completely differently to what was intended by the instigator of the touch (Zur, & Nordmarken, 2018). Kertay and Reviere (1998) state that "if the therapeutic alliance is fragile . . . touch is less likely to be helpful and more likely to be interpreted as aggressive or seductive" (p. 27). This indicates that unless the therapeutic relationship is well established, physical contact would not be appropriate.

Psychologists' perception

A qualitative study of clinical psychologists' perspectives on the use of touch (Harrison, Jones, & Huws, 2012) reflects the numerous dilemmas faced by psychologists in the consideration of touch. Most participants acknowledged the positive impact touch may have but were also mindful of potential risks associated with touch and therefore used touch rarely in their practice. Nevertheless, there may be times within therapy that a hug seems appropriate to the clinical psychologist, for example at times of deep grief on the part of the client. Pope et al. (1987) found over 95% of psychologists in their sample believed that under rare circumstances, hugging a client is ethical.

However, Gutheil and Brodsky (2008) state that "there are virtually no circumstances in which it is appropriate for a therapist to initiate a hug with a patient" (p. 167). They believe that a psychologist should hug a client only when it is initiated by the client, and this should be limited to exceptional circumstances. Nonetheless, this is a difficult issue and rejecting a hug from a client may not seem an appropriate course of action. Declining to return an embrace may cause offence, and possibly even a therapeutic rupture. The clinical psychologist should use his/her own clinical judgement at such times to decide whether a physical embrace would be appropriate.

Recommendations for clinical practice

Setting boundaries

Being explicit and transparent about physical contact from the outset may enable the psychologist and his/her client to reach an agreement regarding the boundaries for his/her relationship. This should therefore help the psychologist to act in the client's best interests regarding the use of physical contact.

Given that the clinical psychologist is responsible for maintaining boundaries safely, the limits of physical contact should perhaps form part of the psychological contract agreed with the client at the outset of therapy. Initiating a discussion about physical contact, amongst other issues, at the outset of therapy may help the client understand the boundaries of the therapeutic relationship and enable him/her to feel more comfortable in what may be, for him/her, an unfamiliar situation. The psychologist can seek to understand his/her client's views regarding physical contact and whether touch is potentially indicated as part of the therapy.

However, a discussion about physical contact on first meeting a client may not feel comfortable for either party. Working with people with a learning disability, I am very aware of the power imbalance and to start a therapeutic relationship with a set of rules may not be appropriate. Instead I tend to see how the relationship progresses and take my lead from them. If he/she is a tactile person then I will ensure we discuss this and set out when touch is acceptable, depending on the individual needs of the client. The needs of the client will also determine when this conversation is appropriate to have, as I would want to ensure we have a good enough rapport to withstand this, but I would also want to be proactive in addressing any potential issues.

Addressing physical contact in the therapeutic relationship

Following on from this, it is advised that any instance of physical contact should be discussed within the therapeutic setting with the client after it has occurred. However, a study by Stenzel and Rupert (2004) suggests that nearly half of over 400 psychologists they surveyed *rarely* or *never* discussed physical contact with their clients. It would seem prudent to discuss instances of physical contact as they occur as this may alleviate any potential threats to the therapeutic alliance, such as the touch being misconstrued by either the client or the psychologist. Failing to openly discuss and resolve acts of physical contact may create a rupture in the therapeutic alliance, resulting in an unsatisfactory outcome to therapy or even accusations of improper conduct by the client to the psychologist. Being transparent about physical contact with a client may reduce such risks and might even facilitate a deeper, more comfortable therapeutic relationship. Transparency may also encourage a shared ownership of the boundaries of the therapeutic relationship, where the client is as concerned with maintaining these as the therapist.

In some instances however, such a discussion may not be feasible due to the client's level of understanding, for example when working with young children or clients with a severe learning disability. Working with clients who cannot generally give informed consent, or perhaps even understand boundaries, carries additional difficulties when considering the use of physical contact. The clinical judgement of the psychologist regarding touch in such situations should be clearly based on the client's needs: Durana (1998) writes that "when in doubt, it is best not to touch" (p. 274). Occasionally however, clinical psychologists are forced to manage unplanned physical contact, for example when a hug is initiated by a client. No guidance offers advice on managing such a situation, so the responsibility of the psychologist in this instance may simply be to act in what he/she believes are the best interests of his/her client at that time and seek supervision.

Seeking guidance

Accessing supervision or consultation with colleagues would be advisable for psychologists using or experiencing physical contact with clients. Pope and Keith-Spiegel (2008) state "consulting with trusted colleagues – those not involved with the situation – can strengthen ethical decision making" (p. 641). Supervision may aid psychologists to reflect on their use of physical contact, perhaps developing a deeper understanding of themselves and their clients along with a greater awareness of significant contextual factors.

As a trainee clinical psychologist, it may be difficult to discuss touch with supervisors given their evaluative role. However, developing a safe space within supervision for such discussions would aid in the development of the trainee's ethical decision-making and professional identity. With growing experience my anxiety regarding touch has reduced and I feel able to use my clinical judgement with more confidence to consider each situation as it arises.

Conclusion

There are many factors to be considered when contemplating whether physical contact is appropriate or not. These factors include the theoretical orientation of the psychologist; contextual factors such as gender, power and culture and the strength of the therapeutic relationship. The lack of professional or organisational guidance regarding physical contact with clients reflects the need for psychologists to use their clinical judgement to make ethical decisions that are in the best interests of their clients. When making such decisions, remaining transparent with clients and colleagues/supervisors regarding use of physical contact may help to encourage well-considered clinical judgements and ensure safer working practices for all.

Note

1 Specific therapies that include touch are not discussed in this chapter, for example Body Psychotherapy (Marlock, Weiss, Young, & Soth, 2015).

Suggested further reading

Westland, G. (2011). Physical touch in psychotherapy: Why are we not touching more? *Body, Movement and Dance in Psychotherapy*, *6*(1), 17–29. doi:10.1080/17432979.20 10.508597

Wosket, V. (2017). Breaking the rules in counselling. In V. Wosket (Ed.), *The therapeutic use of self: Counselling practice, research and supervision* (pp. 133–162). Oxon, UK: Routledge.

Zur, O. (2007). Touch in therapy and the standard of care in psychotherapy and counselling: Bringing clarity to illusive relationships. *United States Association of Body Psychotherapists Journal*, *6*(2), 61–93. Retrieved from www.zurinstitute.com/touch_ standardofcare.pdf

References

Bonitz, V. (2008). Use of physical touch in the "talking cure": A journey to the outskirts of psychotherapy. *Psychotherapy: Theory, Research, Practice, Training*, *45*(3), 391–404. doi:10.1037/a0013311

Borys, D. S., & Pope, K. S. (1989). Dual relationships between therapist and client: A national study of psychologists, psychiatrists and social workers. *Professional Psychology: Research and Practice*, *20*(5), 283–293. doi:10.1037/0735-7028.20.5.283

British Psychological Society. (2009). *Code of ethics and conduct*. Retrieved from www. bps.org.uk/sites/default/files/documents/code_of_ethics_and_conduct.pdf

Calmes, S. A., Piazza, N. J., & Laux, J. M. (2013). The use of touch in counselling: An ethical decision-making model. *Counselling and Values*, *58*(1), 59–68. doi:10.1002/ j.2161-007X.2013.00025.x

Clance, P. R., & Petras, V. J. (1998). Therapists' recall of their decision-making processes regarding the use of touch in ongoing psychotherapy: A preliminary study. In E. W. L. Smith, P. R. Clance, & S. Imes (Eds.), *Touch in psychotherapy* (pp. 92–108). New York, NY: The Guilford Press.

Durana, C. (1998). The use of touch in psychotherapy: Ethical and clinical guidelines. *Psychotherapy: Theory, Research, Practice, Training*, *35*(2), 269–280. doi:10.1037/h0087817

Gutheil, T. G., & Brodsky, A. (2008). *Preventing boundary violations in clinical practice*. New York, NY: The Guilford Press.

Gutheil, T. G., & Gabbard, G. O. (1993). The concept of boundaries in clinical practice: Theoretical and risk-management dimensions. *The American Journal of Psychiatry*, *150*(2), 188–196. doi:10.1176/ajp.150.2.188

Harrison, C., Jones, R. S. P., & Huws, J. C. (2012). "We're people who don't touch": Exploring clinical psychologists' perspectives on their use of touch in therapy. *Counselling Psychology Quarterly*, *25*(3), 277–287. doi:10.1080/09515070.2012.671595

Health and Care Professions Council. (2016). *Standards of conduct, performance and ethics*. Retrieved from www.hcpc-uk.org/publications/standards/index.asp?id=38

Kertay, L., & Reviere, S. L. (1998). Touch in context. In E. W. L. Smith, P. R. Clance, & S. Imes (Eds.), *Touch in psychotherapy* (pp. 16–35). New York, NY: The Guilford Press.

Marlock, G., Weiss, H., Young, C., & Soth, M. (2015). *The handbook of body psychotherapy and somatic psychology*. Berkeley, CA: North Atlantic Books.

McNeil-Haber, F. M. (2004). Ethical considerations in the use of nonerotic touch in psychotherapy with children. *Ethics & Behaviour*, *14*(2), 123–140. doi:10.1207/ s15327019eb1402_3

Pope, K. S., & Keith-Spiegel, P. (2008). A practical approach to boundaries in psychotherapy: Making decisions, bypassing blunders, and mending fences. *Journal of Clinical Psychology: In Session, 64*(5), 638–652. doi:10.1002/jclp.20477

Pope, K. S., Tabachnick, B. G., & Keith-Spiegel, P. (1987). Ethics of practice: The beliefs and behaviours of psychologists as therapists. In D. N. Bersoff (Ed.), *Ethical conflicts in psychology* (4th ed., pp. 74–90). Washington, DC: American Psychological Association.

Reamer, F. G. (2017). Ethical and risk management issues in the use of touch. In J. A. Courtney & R. D. Nolan (Eds.), *Touch in child counselling and play therapy: An ethical and clinical guide* (pp. 18–32). New York, NY: Routledge.

Smith, E. W. L. (1998). A taxonomy and ethics of touch in psychotherapy. In E. W. L. Smith, P. R. Clance, & S. Imes (Eds.), *Touch in psychotherapy* (pp. 36–51). New York, NY: The Guilford Press.

Stenzel, C. L., & Rupert, P. A. (2004). Psychologists' use of touch in individual psychotherapy. *Psychotherapy: Theory, Research, Practice, Training, 41*(3), 332–345. doi:10. 1037/0033-3204.41.3.332

Zur, O. (2007). Touch in therapy and the standard of care in psychotherapy and counselling: Bringing clarity to illusive relationships. *United States Association of Body Psychotherapists Journal, 6*(2), 61–93. Retrieved from www.zurinstitute.com/touch_standardofcare.pdf

Zur, O., & Nordmarken, N. (2018). *To touch or not to touch: Exploring the myth of prohibition on touch in psychotherapy and counselling.* Retrieved from www.zurinstitute.com/touchintherapy.html

Chapter 3

Working in secure settings

How has this influenced the development of a professional identity?

Laura Cramond and Ailsa Lord

Summary points

- Forensic settings can present many challenges to working therapeutically.
- Clinical psychologists are well placed to negotiate these challenges and support the work of other professionals in these settings.
- The challenges encountered by the authors have shaped their clinical practice in other fields.

Background

Both authors came into clinical psychology training from forensic settings, including a secure hospital for people with intellectual disabilities (AL), and a prison and secure hospital settings for people experiencing interpersonal difficulties (LC). Forensic services offer assessment, intervention and care within a secure setting for individuals who have been convicted of criminal offences (or are at serious risk of doing so), with or without diagnosed mental health difficulties, with the aim of reducing risk to the individual and the public (Joint Commissioning Panel for Mental Health, 2013).

AL's experience of working in secure services involved engaging service users in comprehensive post-admission assessments, the results of which informed a service user's pathway and guided appropriate interventions to reduce offending behaviour upon discharge into the community. Interventions included one-to-one anger management, understanding and managing emotions groups and group sex offender treatment programmes, which ran on a rolling programme throughout the year, led by members of the psychology department and often delivered alongside multidisciplinary colleagues.

LC's experience of working in prison and secure hospitals involved assessments of psychological wellbeing and risk for clinical and research purposes. Participants were recruited for research projects, and the role involved administering relevant questionnaires and conducting qualitative interviews. Clinically, the role also involved contributing to assessment and formulation using psychometrics and risk assessment tools to inform service user care pathways. Services advocated a strong sense of collaboration and recovery, however this was within predefined structures of the mental health and criminal justice systems.

In this chapter, we will consider how the challenges faced in these settings influenced our professional identity as we progressed through clinical psychology training to become qualified clinical psychologists. We are by no means experts in the forensic field, having both chosen to work in different areas since qualifying (AL in older adult mental health and LC in physical health). However we feel our experiences have been influential in the development of our transferable skills and are invaluable in all the settings we have worked in since. We will discuss our reflections on motivation, coercion, collaboration and decision-making about risk management in forensic settings and consider how these challenges have shaped our practice.

Challenges to therapeutic intervention

Person-centred care has long been a guiding principle for clinicians working in and social care settings (e.g., Department of Health [DoH], 2013; The Health Foundation, 2014) and as clinical psychologists we endeavour to ensure service users' voices are heard and understood by our colleagues and other stakeholders. Service user choice and collaborative working are crucial to this, and the British Psychological Society (BPS, 2008) indicates that clinical psychologists must act within the best interests of the service users they support. Forensic settings can challenge this, as a result of the inherent power imbalance between staff and service users (Mason & Adler, 2012).

By the nature of detention, a service user's opportunities for choice are somewhat restricted, making him/her potentially more vulnerable to coercive practice and more likely to engage in interventions because of the potential liberties it affords him/her. While this is certainly not true of all service users, some may engage in interventions due to external rather than internal motivations, such as extra incentives and privileges such as escorted leave (Mason & Adler, 2012; Sainsbury Centre for Mental Health, 2008), and one-to-one time with the therapist. Such coercive environments can challenge our attempts to remain person-centred.

During our time in forensic settings, we noticed that service users seemed to be prescribed psychological interventions, their suitability for which was decided based on a limited number of factors (often related to their forensic history). The reduction of potential reoffending via the provision of offence-focused and mandated interventions is a main priority of detention, which is guided by an evidence base (Blud, Travers, Nugent, & Thornton, 2010) and aims to reduce the rate of reoffending (Duncan, Nicol, Ager, & Dalgleish, 2006). However, our experience was that service users would frequently disengage from interventions, as described by Olver, Stockdale and Wormith (2011). Now, working in settings where we can develop more idiosyncratic formulations, we reflect on our time in forensic settings and realise how challenging it was to meet service users' best interests, given the lack of choice around intervention, a lack of flexibility in how it is offered, or indeed the lack of choice around whether to engage or not.

This power differential between staff and service users is particularly important to consider in forensic settings, especially where service users may be coerced into engaging with psychological interventions. The requirement to complete an offence-focused intervention to satisfy the conditions of a service user's detention is often a driver for this, and the service users are often required to demonstrate cognitive and/or behavioural change which suggests reduced risk of recidivism and therefore readiness for discharge. However, it is neither consistent with our ethical principles (BPS, 2008) nor person-centred to coerce someone to engage in intervention or to only offer mandated generic options that are not formulation-driven and tailored to meet individual needs.

Drawing on therapeutic models to negotiate challenges

We have found that those who seem to benefit most from therapeutic input are people who have actively chosen to engage in therapy, often having considered what they might want to make sense of or change, and those where decisions about therapy have been made collaboratively. As we have built on our forensic experience, we have learned the value of investing additional time to develop a therapeutic relationship, so that we can best understand our service users and work on potential barriers to change, with a view to achieving longer-term benefits for their recovery.

Johnstone (2017) describes formulation as a structure for thinking together with service users about how to understand their experiences and how to move forward. To ensure that intervention is not simply a tick-box exercise and is delivered at the right time for each service user, we can use formulation to understand what is important to them. We can support them to make informed decisions which are consistent with their life values, taking into consideration the potential longer-term impact of such interventions. In forensic settings, this might require focusing on readiness to engage in mandated interventions and how to maintain changes made, or understanding the underlying relational patterns which may contribute to the maintenance of service users' difficulties and offending behaviour.

Clinical psychologists are trained to draw on various models of therapy and are encouraged to be integrative in their work (BPS, 2011). We are acutely aware that interventions are not 'one size fits all', particularly as we often work with layers of complexity which may be influenced by issues specific to our population groups (e.g., transitions in later life, adjustment to physical health difficulties) and where a potentially manualised intervention requires adaptations.

A framework which might be helpful in preparing service users for mandated interventions is Prochaska and DiClemente's (1982) *Stages of Change* model, which is the basis for motivational interviewing techniques (Miller & Rollnick, 2002). For example, enrolling a service user at the pre-contemplation stage into an anger management program may be fruitless, as engagement may be superficial and motivated by external factors. A better approach would be to support the individual to consider where he/she is at now and how therapeutic intervention might be useful to him/her. Someone who has moved from a pre-contemplative to a contemplative stage may understand how the intervention might be useful, but might need support to consider the costs and benefits of changing to enhance his/her readiness. It is only when a service user reaches a point of readiness towards action that intervention is likely to be of longer-term benefit (Day, Bryan, Davey, & Casey, 2007; Yong, Williams, Provan, Clarke, & Sinclair, 2015).

Acceptance and commitment therapy (ACT; Hayes, Luoma, Bond, Masuda, & Lillis, 2006) approaches could also aid service users in making decisions regarding engagement, intervention choice and behaviour change by drawing on their values. Clinical psychologists might undertake preliminary work to support service users to identify the gains and costs of possible choices or directions, such as engaging in intervention, thinking about difficult issues and choosing alternative behaviours. This might be guided by therapeutic discussions of what is important to them within the context of their life. In forensic settings, motivations to engage in interventions might include a service user's desire to change his/her situation, develop better relationships with others, have greater liberties, or to avoid reoffending. These goals might be underpinned by core values the person feels he/she holds, such as feeling connected to others, or a sense of pride or achievement. ACT approaches might help a person consider how he/she could live his/her life more in keeping with these values, in a collaborative way which helps him/her to identify goals that are meaningful to him/her. Understanding the potentially counterproductive nature of enforced therapy has helped us to better meet the needs of our clients in our current settings, and has led us to question referrals lacking consent, spending more time on pre-therapy work if necessary, and accepting when people choose not to engage.

These reflections have been invaluable in shaping our professional identities and approach to working therapeutically with service users. We consider and allow time to collaboratively explore motivators and barriers to change, as well as hopes and expectations with service users. This includes identifying reasons for accessing the service, such as individuals feeling they should engage in therapy, being told to see the psychologist by other professionals or hoping that intervention will be a quick fix. Alternatively, difficult feelings around intervention can be explored, such as seeing psychology as a last resort, believing that others think difficulties are 'all in their head', or beliefs around talking about difficulties equating to being weak. We are then able to work with these issues before an individual decides whether to engage in therapy that he/she may not want or need, or feel able to engage in.

Challenges regarding risk management

Risk management is another priority for forensic services, who must balance the potential benefits of positive risk taking with their duty to protect the public.

DoH (2013) describe a need for a balance between empowerment, safeguarding, choice and risk. Clinical psychologists in these settings have a dual role: being a therapist while also managing risk. This may have implications on the development of a good therapeutic relationship, as the psychologist may have to make recommendations or take actions that the service user disagrees with.

Formulation-informed risk assessment, planning and management can reduce risk-aversive cultures by offering an evidence base for taking positive risks for service users as well as having wider organisational and systemic influences. We often found risk to be considered without the service user present in forensic settings, which reinforces the inherent power imbalances described earlier. Collaborative and transparent risk planning can enable us to work more effectively within service constraints and requirements (BPS, 2011). This can incorporate the risks posed by service users to themselves, to others and from others, as well as those factors that protect against risk.

A large part of our current roles within multidisciplinary teams is consultation with our colleagues, during which we can share formulations to aid care-planning and provide a clinical rationale for any decisions which are made. Our experiences in forensic services have shaped our approach to risk management in other settings. We still have a responsibility to protect the client and public from harm, but can use our relationships with clients to have open and honest conversations about how to manage risk in a proactive and positive way.

Challenges using clinical supervision

Supervision is essential in developing the confidence to work with issues such as power imbalance, readiness to change, collaboration and managing risk, and is something that we have highly valued pre- and post-qualification. Regular clinical supervision ensures that we have adequate space to discuss and reflect on our work and to have that work considered by another professional (BPS, 2008). The ability to effectively use supervision, comprehend supervision models and understand their contribution to practice is a standard of proficiency for practitioner psychologists (Health and Care Professions Council, 2010). When working in forensic settings, we found clinical supervision to be crucial in understanding the influence of power in both individual and group work, as well as how this operated on a wider systemic level. Whilst clinical supervision is essential to our roles (BPS, 2006), we believe that reflection should also be an ongoing process throughout therapeutic sessions. Our experiences of supervision in forensic settings have certainly influenced our approach to working reflectively in our qualified roles. For example, we have recognised that supervision and reflection is not always available to or prioritised by other professional groups. We have explored ways to promote reflection on professional and ethical issues, including the provision of psychologically informed reflective practice groups and supervision, which we believe could be a valuable resource in forensic services.

Conclusion

While there are numerous challenges inherent to working within the constraints of forensic settings, which may not always sit comfortably with our ethical position as clinical psychologists, we believe there are many ways we can use our skills to promote collaborative working, address potential power imbalances and take clinically informed positive risks with service users. Our experiences of working in forensic settings have undoubtedly shaped our professional identity and afforded us invaluable insight into issues of collaboration, coercion and risk management outside of forensic services.

Suggested further reading

Davies, J., & Nagi, C. (Eds.). (2017). *Individual psychological therapies in forensic settings: Research and practice*. London: Routledge.

Sturmey, P., & McMurran, M. (Eds.). (2011). *Forensic case formulation*. Chichester: Wiley-Blackwell.

References

Blud, L., Travers, R., Nugent, F., & Thornton, D. (2010). Accreditation of offending behaviour programmes in HM prison service: 'What works' in practice. *Legal and Criminological Psychology*, *8*(1), 69–81. doi:10.1348/135532503762871255

British Psychological Society (BPS). (2006). *Core competencies – Clinical psychology – A guide*. Leicester: British Psychological Society.

British Psychological Society (BPS). (2008). *Generic professional practice guidelines*. Retrieved from www.bps.org.uk/sites/default/files/documents/generic_professional_practice_guidelines.pdf

British Psychological Society (BPS). (2011). *Good practice guidelines on the use of psychological formulation*. Retrieved from https://www1.bps.org.uk/system/files/Public%20files/DCP/cat-842.pdf

Day, A., Bryan, J., Davey, L., & Casey, S. (2007). The process of change in offender rehabilitation programmes. *Psychology, Crime & Law*, *12*(5), 473–487. doi:10.1080/10683160500151209

Department of Health. (2013). *Integrated care: Our shared commitment*. Retrieved from www.gov.uk/government/uploads/system/uploads/attachment_data/file/287815/DEFINITIVE_FINAL_VERSION_Integrated_Care_and_Support_-_Our_Shared_Commitment_2013-05-13.pdf

Duncan, E. A., Nicol, M. M., Ager, A., & Dalgleish, L. (2006). A systematic review of structured group interventions with mentally disordered offenders. *Criminal Behaviour and Mental Health*, *16*(4), 217–241. doi:10.1002/cbm.631

Hayes, S. C., Luoma, J., Bond, F., Masuda, A., & Lillis, J. (2006). Acceptance and commitment therapy: Model, processes, and outcomes. *Behaviour Research and Therapy*, *44*(1), 1–25. doi:10.1016/j.brat.2005.06.006

Health and Care Professions Council. (2010). *Standards of proficiency – Practitioner psychologists*. London: Health and Care Professions Council. Retrieved from www.hcpc-uk.org/assets/documents/10002963SOP_Practitioner_psychologists.pdf

Johnstone, L. (2017). Psychological formulation as an alternative to psychiatric diagnosis. *Journal of Humanistic Psychology, 58*(1), 30–46. doi:10.1177/0022167817722230

Joint Commissioning Panel for Mental Health. (2013). *Guidance for commissioners of forensic mental health services.* Retrieved from www.rcpsych.ac.uk/pdf/jcpmh-forensic-guide.pdf

Mason, K., & Adler, J. R. (2012). Group-work therapeutic engagement in high secure hospital: Male service-user perspectives. *The British Journal of Forensic Practice, 14*, 92–103. doi:10.1108/14636641211223657

Miller, W. R., & Rollnick, S. (2002). *Motivational interviewing: Preparing people for change* (2nd ed.). New York, NY: Guilford Press.

Olver, M. E., Stockdale, K. C., & Wormith, J. S. (2011). A meta-analysis of predictors of offender treatment attrition and its relationship to recidivism. *Journal of Consulting and Clinical Psychology, 79*(1), 6–21. doi:10.1037/a0022200

Prochaska, J. O., & DiClemente, C. C. (1982). Transtheoretical therapy: Toward a more integrative model of change. *Psychotherapy: Theory, Research & Practice, 19*(3), 276–288. doi:10.1037/h0088437

Sainsbury Centre for Mental Health. (2008). *A review of the use of offending behaviour programmes for people with mental health problems.* Retrieved from www.patient library.net/tempgen/22802.pdf

The Health Foundation. (2014). *Person-centred care made simple: What everyone should know about person-centred care.* Retrieved from www.health.org.uk/sites/health/files/PersonCentredCareMadeSimple.pdf

Yong, A. D., Williams, M., Provan, H., Clarke, D., & Sinclair, G. (2015). How do offenders move through the stages of change? *Psychology, Crime & Law, 21*(4), 375–397. doi:10.1080/1068316X.2014.989166

Chapter 4

Prescribed endings in therapy during clinical psychology training

Sarah Savekar

Summary points

- Prescribed endings in therapy, as dictated by time-limited clinical placements, can lead to problems within a therapeutic relationship and will negatively impact clients if not managed appropriately.
- Endings should be discussed at the outset of a therapeutic intervention to ensure that the client knows what to expect and to help set a clear agenda for therapy.
- A well-managed ending can be incredibly beneficial for clients, and both therapist and client should seek to be open about their emotional responses to this.

The inevitability of endings in therapy can be both powerful and problematic. Prescribed endings in therapy are a recurring issue throughout clinical psychology training, yet these experiences provide opportunities for critical reflection on how we can manage ethical issues positively to support the people we are working with to make positive changes. As a trainee clinical psychologist, learning to manage these scenarios effectively is a crucial aspect of developing a professional identity.

Prescribed endings occur both through training and beyond. For example, primary care therapy services in the NHS often dictate the number of sessions that therapists can offer based on service provision, and people who are inpatients on adult mental health wards can be discharged with little warning. Clinical psychologists have to be increasingly flexible when working in fast-paced, resource-limited services as members of multidisciplinary teams.

As a trainee clinical psychologist however, endings are sometimes prescribed by programme and service demands; sometimes therapeutic work comes to an end due to the placement finishing rather than a natural ending. Trainees traditionally spend six months working on each core placement, during which they manage a clinical caseload under supervision in order to gain a breadth of experience and develop the required competencies set out by the Health and Care Professions Council (HCPC, 2009). People working therapeutically with trainee clinical psychologists therefore have a prescribed ending to the therapeutic relationship from the outset. There are both opportunities and obstacles associated with prescribed endings and this will be discussed in light of existing literature and current policy informing practice as well as personal reflections.

Best practice guidance provided by the Department of Health (DoH; Roth & Pilling, 2007) regarding the competencies required to deliver cognitive-behavioural therapy to people with depression and anxiety highlights the importance of managing the end of treatment. The guidelines emphasise that engaging with this process is an integral part of managing the therapeutic relationship, offering specific advice on discussing the ending early on within therapy, and reviewing how the client might manage post-therapy. This chapter will reflect on some of the issues inherent to these processes.

Personal reflections on a clinical example

During a placement in a physical health psychology service in the NHS, I was working with a client who had been referred due to difficulties coming to terms with her physical symptoms and anxiety following some recent surgery. I have used the pseudonym Mary and changed some details in order to maintain confidentiality. The scope of the psychology input available in this service was short-term work, focused on health-related issues. Therefore, challenges arose when people who accessed the service also had pre-existing emotional difficulties, as the health psychology service was only commissioned to offer short-term psychological input for health-related issues. It was necessary to be explicit about what would be achievable in a health psychology service, and to determine when someone may benefit from input from further longer-term input from a community mental health service.

During the assessment process, it became evident that Mary had experienced a difficult attachment history, characterised by rejection from other people. She disclosed long-term relationship and emotional difficulties, and we discussed how her vulnerability during her significant ill health and surgery had triggered further relational instability and distress. Mary highlighted her discomfort and dissatisfaction at how the fixed duration of the placement impacted on the end of her therapy. It was evident early on that Mary would benefit from longer-term input from mental health services to support her to explore her past experiences and the impact of this on her today; a brief number of sessions would not provide the scope or containment to begin this type of work and it fell outside of the remit of what the health psychology service was commissioned to offer. However, the current issues that Mary was facing were inextricably linked to her past experiences.

At the outset of our first meeting, Mary and I discussed the remit of the service and my role as a trainee. We talked about how our work together would be time limited and would focus on specific health-related problems.

I spent some time thinking about both Mary's feelings about this situation, and my own response to the ending of our therapeutic work. My initial reaction was a feeling of unease, as I was aware that Mary might experience the end of therapy as an abandonment, and that this might reinforce her beliefs about herself and others.

I worried she may feel that she was not going to be given enough time to achieve her therapeutic goals and that the scope of the service was not what she needed. Feeling responsible for the prescribed ending to therapy made me uncomfortable; if I were not offering the work as a trainee on placement and had instead been employed as a permanent member of staff, might Mary have had the option of continuing her sessions for longer? Is the end of the placement a justifiable reason to bring a therapeutic intervention to a close?

I reflected on these feelings and my sense of responsibility in supervision. This helped me to recognise the importance of discussing these concerns with Mary. Mary and I explored her emotions in relation to the end of therapy in an open and transparent way. We used an approach based on *compassion-focused therapy* (Gilbert, 2010), which draws from a range of disciplines such as evolutionary psychology, biology, neuroscience and Eastern philosophy. Paul Gilbert (2010) proposes that by applying principles of compassion to the self and to others, then we can relieve distress linked to core feelings of shame and patterns of self-criticism. We used the *in vivo* situation of the prescribed ending to therapy as a therapeutic anchor from which to work from; enabling us to think about applying principles of self-compassion to times when she was feeling let down; acknowledging the very real feelings that these experiences had triggered, but also trying to find positive and practical ways to manage these often overwhelming emotions.

Indeed, this prescribed ending allowed us to be more explicit about identifying therapeutic goals and priorities. The aim of these sessions became about supporting Mary to learn to care for herself and self-soothe. We discussed Mary's feelings within the context of a wider formulation, which helped her to make sense of her understandable and justifiable feelings of abandonment. We agreed that, if our work was going to be brief, Mary's priority was the recent surgery and how she was managing the overwhelming feelings and distress around her physical symptoms. This also gave us the opportunity to use a compassion-focused approach as preparation for future therapy work within mental health services, focusing on the longstanding issues she continued to struggle with. For example, we discussed managing feelings between sessions, recognising when the threat system is being activated, good self-care and experiencing within therapy the challenge of being open about her thoughts and emotions. Collaboration was key in establishing the agenda and aims of therapy. Discussing the ending from the beginning was vital to this process.

To support the referral to mental health services, with Mary's consent, I contacted a clinical psychologist in the service I was referring to. This psychologist used cognitive-analytic therapy (Ryle & Kerr, 2003), which is a particularly helpful approach when working relationally with someone who has experienced disrupted attachments in early life. Communicating with the clinical psychologist working in mental health services was useful as we were able to discuss the benefits of the brief work Mary and I had done in relation to her physical health problems. This helped facilitate continuity of care, which enabled us to tailor support to Mary's needs. Being able to discuss the nature of cognitive-analytic therapy with Mary helped her to understand the potential benefits of this way of working.

Although there was limited time available for our work together, Mary and I identified that this actually helped to ensure that our work was focused with clear goals, enabling us to make progress in line with shared expectations. Liaising with different services and developing relationships with colleagues helped to ensure continuity of care and open channels of communication. This enabled us to provide the most appropriate therapeutic input and support Mary with the transition into another service. Mary was included in the process of referral; she had a clear understanding of what we had been working on and what the plan was for future intervention. I hope that by including Mary in this process of defining a therapeutic pathway, we helped her to feel held in mind by the professionals involved in her care, which was in contrast to many of her previous experiences.

Critical reflections on literature

The research literature surrounding endings is predominantly based on qualitative research and case studies. From an epistemological point of view, quantitative randomised designs may not be the most appropriate method of investigating intricacies of therapeutic process. Quantitative research methods may not be able to measure outcomes when investigating a process, or indeed finding an outcome measure that would have sufficient sensitivity for exploring the complexity of endings. Popay, Rogers and Williams (1998) outline an interesting argument for why qualitative methods are often well suited (and arguably more applicable) in the healthcare arena for these reasons.

Freud described endings as terminations which highlighted feelings of dependency versus wanting to gain independence, offering the opportunity to work through conflict to reach resolutions (Freud, 1914). Though dated in many regards, Freud's assertion here relates to my work with Mary as we focused on the feelings evoked by the ending as a *here and now* example of how she could manage emotion responses and foster self-compassion when feelings of abandonment arise.

I have learned this is a two-way process and that, as a therapist, I can also use a compassionate approach to manage feelings of guilt relating to prescribed endings. I used supervision to help me to think about my own emotional responses to the situation and how they might help me to make sense of Mary's experiences. Paying attention to my feelings of guilt alerted me to the potential countertransference being evoked by Mary's apparent distress at sessions coming to an end. Was this an invitation to rescue? An invitation to halt the abandonment? It enabled me to focus mindfully on how I felt in the therapy room with Mary and what re-enactments I felt pulled into, which may have damaged the therapeutic process and ultimately led to a less-than-optimal outcome.

Types of endings

Wittenberg (1999) describes three different types of therapeutic endings. The first are *natural* endings which occur when the client has developed to a point where he/she can manage without the support of a therapist. He outlines how some therapies which go on too long can infantilise the client (Wittenberg, 1999), therefore highlighting how endings can be positive and empowering. The second are *disruption* endings, which are a result of the client ceasing to attend, for example due to feeling uncomfortable or a disconnection between therapist and client. The last type are *premature* endings which are influenced by external circumstances, such as the service user moving or demands relating to the therapist's career: for example, the end of a training placement.

Planning endings due to fixed timescales rather than presenting difficulties or agreed goals can bring about uncomfortable feelings for both the professional and the client. Offering the service user the opportunity to continue treatment with another professional after the end of the placement may be an option to discuss, if this is appropriate. However, for the client, the prospect of developing a new therapeutic relationship and relaying all of his/her history and difficulties to someone different may feel daunting and tokenistic. Services may also not have the resources to be able to offer this. Maples and Walker (2014) suggest that termination in therapy can be particularly difficult for therapists in training when it is an aversive experience, compared with more experienced therapists who may have encountered and managed these difficulties many times before.

What makes a good ending?

Schlesinger (2005) reflects that clinicians have high expectations of the perfect ending. Of course, in the reality of clinical work this is often not the case. A more pragmatic approach is outlined by Hoffman (1998) and Gabbard (2009) who describe making a *good enough* ending. Drawing on these ideas in relation to the guilt I experienced in relation to Mary's ending helped me to think about my own expectations, and the extent to which these were similar to Mary's perceptions on how the piece of work should conclude. I have learned the benefits of planning ahead and having conversations about endings at the outset of any therapeutic intervention, in order to discuss the client's expectations of how the work might finish. Although this sounds simple, the client's perspective on this is rarely sought.

Indeed, Råbu, Binder and Haavind (2013) highlight that most of the existing empirical research in relation to therapeutic endings is only from the therapist's perspective. They conducted a qualitative investigation which involved interviewing clients and therapists about endings, in order to explore the process of achieving good enough endings. They found that good enough endings occurred when the therapist and client made combined efforts to work through points of tension associated with ending, recognising the continuing bond that may go beyond the end of the intervention. Despite the limitations of this study (for example, the sample consisting of people who had positive experiences of therapy and therapists being aware of the study focus on endings) it offers interesting insights into this process.

A continuing bond could be characterised by an open discharge, or the offer of a follow-up appointment arranged in the future. I continue to employ this strategy from training in my qualified work, as a way of supporting people to feel empowered by their skills but with the added reassurance of one last appointment if needed as a booster session. A follow-up session usually includes a review of strategies and a solution-focused discussion of the interim time since the end of therapy. Of course, the client has the option to decline the session if he/she feels that things are going well or the follow-up is not required; offering this choice can be therapeutic in itself. Due to the structured time boundaries of a training placement, this may need to be factored in from the start of therapy.

Principles of attachment theory are also relevant to considering how we might best manage prescribed endings with people who may have difficult relational histories. The difficulties Mary described may be consistent with descriptions of an anxious and preoccupied adult attachment style (Ainsworth, 1989). Mary had reportedly been abandoned and rejected by caregivers from an early age and grew up in an environment in which affection was withheld. She identified that, as a result, she now seeks intimacy over autonomy in her relationships with others.

This style of attachment may be particularly relevant when considering therapeutic endings, as the prescribed ending may be perceived as abandonment and reinforce negative beliefs such as *I'm not worthy of being cared for by anyone* or *They don't want to see me anymore, there's something wrong with me* (Howe, 2011). Feelings of uncertainty about the relationship may be experienced by the client. Behaviours which serve to prolong the relationship may occur, such as increased self-harm and risk-related behaviours, or the raising of difficult topics at the end of a session. Although challenging, this may offer a therapeutic advantage as the therapist has a here and now example to work on with the client, and an opportunity to model a good ending and explore the re-enactment of relational patterns as they occur. A well-managed prescribed ending can help to explore, address and reshape such attachment styles.

Within my clinical supervision, we formulated both Mary's responses and my own emotional reactions to providing a good enough ending. Through doing this, I was able to take a step back from the situation and identify that my responsibility was managing a good ending for Mary and supporting her transition into mental health services for ongoing support. A good prescribed ending in Mary's case served as an opportunity for her to experience a tolerable ending that was well prepared for, while hopefully modelling a healthier way of ending a relationship and demonstrating ways to manage associated emotions. I also reflected that even an ending at a later date may have prompted the same difficulties, and while thinking about the ending of the placement had triggered this reaction, similar feelings may have arisen even if this had not been a factor in suggesting an onward referral. Reflecting on and disentangling my own emotional reactions from Mary's was helpful in successfully navigating my discussions with her in our sessions.

Conclusion

Thinking about endings in therapy enabled me to develop as a trainee clinical psychologist, helping me to consider ongoing issues relating to individual client needs within the context of service demands and real-world complexities. I have learned that prescribed endings as a trainee are inevitable; however, by being mindful of our own feelings and those of the person we are working with, we can support a safe and empowering ending. This can be achieved by good preparation, including outlining time limitations and expectations around this from the outset. In order for change to occur within such time-focused work, it is beneficial to be focused and to set realistic, achievable goals. The small changes achievable within such brief work can make a big difference to someone's psychological wellbeing and daily functioning, even within the context of complex and long-standing difficulties.

I have learned that, as my professional identity has developed, it is important to engage with the principles that we share with our clients. For example, I try to integrate a compassionate approach in reflecting on my own feelings about my work with clients and to explore the emotions I experience surrounding endings, to help me to think about potential countertransference and the relational pulls to offer more sessions when this might not be helpful, to fix or to rescue the client. Clinical supervision is a good place to reflect on these processes and to discuss how these principles apply.

Although this chapter has focused on prescribed endings as a trainee clinical psychologist, this is also relevant post-qualification. Within the context of increasing pressures on the NHS, endings may become increasingly prescribed due to service demands, limitations on resources, financial costs, long waiting lists and other pressures. The experience of working with these issues throughout training is important in enabling clinical psychologists to engage with such challenges in a positive and pro-active way. Where appropriate, it can be helpful to offer interventions even when they are brief and time-limited; as long as this does not inadvertently cause distress. Reflecting on these issues has also helped me to realise the importance of being able to effectively differentiate when a person is in need of further, longer-term input, based on a clear and robust formulation and intervention plan.

Suggested further reading

Bennett, D., & Parry, G. (2004). Maintaining the therapeutic alliance: Resolving alliance-threatening interactions related to the transference. In D. Charman (Ed.), *Core processes in brief psychodynamic psychotherapy: Advancing effective practice* (pp. 251–272). New Jersey: Lawrence Erlbaum Associates.

Malan, D. (1995). *Individual psychotherapy and the science of psychodynamics*. Florida: CRC Press.

Ryle, A., Poynton, A. M., & Brockman, B. J. (1990). *Cognitive-analytic therapy: Active participation in change: A new integration in brief psychotherapy*. Chichester: John Wiley & Sons.

References

Ainsworth, M. S. (1989). Attachments beyond infancy. *American Psychologist, 44*(4), 709–716. doi:10.1037/0003-066X.44.4.709

Freud, S. (1914). Remembering, repeating and working-through. In J. Strachey (Ed. & Trans.), *The Standard edition of the complete psychological works of Sigmund Freud* (Vol. 3, pp. 147–156). London: Hogarth Press.

Gabbard, G. O. (2009). What is a "good enough" termination? *Journal of the American Psychoanalytic Association, 57*(3), 575–594. doi:10.1177/0003065109340678

Gilbert, P. (2010). *Compassion focused therapy: Distinctive features.* London: Routledge.

Health and Care Professions Council. (2009). *Standards of proficiency – Practitioner Psychologists.* London: HCPC.

Hoffman, I. Z. (1998). *Ritual and spontaneity in the psychoanalytic process. A dialectical-constructivist view.* Hillsdale, NJ: Analytic Press.

Howe, D. (2011). *Attachment across the life course: A brief introduction.* New York, NY: Palgrave Macmillan.

Maples, J. L., & Walker, R. L. (2014). Consolidation rather than termination: Rethinking how psychologists label and conceptualize the final phase of psychological treatment. *Professional Psychology: Research and Practice, 45*(2), 104–110. doi:10.1037/a0036250

Popay, J., Rogers, A., & Williams, G. (1998). Rationale and standards for the systematic review of qualitative literature in health services research. *Qualitative Health Research, 8*(3), 341–351. doi:10.1177/104973239800800305

Råbu, M., Binder, P. E., & Haavind, H. (2013). Negotiating ending: A qualitative study of the process of ending psychotherapy. *European Journal of Psychotherapy & Counselling, 15*(3), 274–295. doi:10.1080/13642537.2013.810962

Roth, A. D., & Pilling, S. (2007). *The competences required to deliver effective cognitive and behavioural therapy for people with depression and with anxiety disorders.* London: Department of Health. Retrieved from http://webarchive.nationalarchives. gov.uk/20130105063655/www.dh.gov.uk/prod_consum_dh/groups/dh_digitalassets/@ dh/@en/documents/digitalasset/dh_078535.pdf

Ryle, A., & Kerr, I. B. (2003). *Introducing cognitive analytic therapy: Principles and practice.* Chichester: John Wiley & Sons.

Schlesinger, H. J. (2005). *Endings and beginnings: On the technique of terminating psychotherapy and psychoanalysis.* Hillsdale, NJ: Analytic Press.

Wittenberg, I. (1999). Ending therapy. *Journal of Child Psychotherapy, 25*(3), 339–356. doi:10.1080/00754179908260300

Part II

Understanding the broader role of clinical psychology

Professional issues across areas of practice

Chapter 5

The identity and contribution of clinical psychology in CAMHS

Graham Simpson-Adkins

Summary points

- Clinical psychologists frequently work in multidisciplinary teams, but despite high demand for the profession, there have been longstanding disputes concerning the unique selling point and distinct contribution offered.
- The role of clinical psychology is complex and multifaceted; which may be a both a strength and a frailty.
- There is an ever-growing need to establish clearly the professional identity of clinical psychology, and to ensure this is more widely and explicitly understood.

Clinical psychology in teams

It is widely considered that multidisciplinary team (MDT) working is an effective, if not fundamental approach for the delivery of many mental health services. For instance, it has been suggested that in child and adolescent mental health services (CAMHS), MDT working improves service quality and outcomes (Department of Health, 2004; Kutash et al., 2014; Miller & Ahmad, 2000; Salmon, 2004). As the world of healthcare has evolved, there has been a persistent drive towards a thorough integration of clinical psychologists into the structure and functioning of these and other mental health teams (British Psychological Society; BPS, 2007). This has meant that, nowadays, clinical psychologists most often work alongside other professional groups, such as psychiatrists, social workers, mental health nurses and psychotherapists. This has, however, resulted in a blurring of many professional boundaries (Cheshire & Pilgrim, 2004).

Consequently, clinical psychology's evolution over the years has needed to advance amongst a political struggle for professional ground with these other professions, particularly psychiatry (Cheshire & Pilgrim, 2004). The need for delineation of a distinctive professional identity has become an increasingly pressing issue over recent years (Division of Clinical Psychology; DCP, 2007). For instance, the introduction of the Agenda for Change has increased the visibility of the higher payment banding of clinical psychologists compared to other mental health professionals with whom we share many roles and responsibilities, particularly in teams, which understandably amplifies the pressure on clinical psychologists to demonstrate value for money (Department of Health, 2003; DCP, 2007). With the move towards commissioner-led services, recurring disputes have ensued concerning the unique selling point and distinctive contribution of clinical psychologists (Christofides, Johnstone, & Musa, 2012).

Plagued by a persistent lack of role clarity

The Understanding Customer Needs of Clinical Psychology Services report (DCP, 2007) brought together the perceptions of service managers and NHS commissioners regarding the profession's strengths and weaknesses. Worryingly, inconsistencies in the perception of value offered by clinical psychologists were highlighted and attention was directed towards a lack of role clarity and expectations. This was proposed as a major perceived weakness of the profession (DCP, 2007).

Despite this lack of certainty, it has been demonstrated that various stakeholders express "an overwhelming preference for the integration of psychologists within teams but only if psychologists retained their unique identity and contribution" (BPS, 2007, p. 3). However, nowhere has it been specified exactly what this unique identity and contribution is. This furthers this trend of confusion, both within and between professions. It appears that clinicians and non-clinicians who work with clinical psychologists are unclear regarding the identity, contribution and value offered by the profession, yet interestingly, continue to desire their presence, particularly in teams. While I feel somewhat comforted by this, I fear that this is not a strong enough foundation on which to solidify our place in the world of healthcare in the future.

How do you solve a problem like a psychologist's identity?

There have been a number of attempts to delineate the professional identity of clinical psychologists. Defining the identity of a profession involves not only the identification of the roles and activities typically recognised and performed by the profession (Lancaster & Smith, 2002), but also the recognition of the features which are *not* performed by other professions (Cheshire & Pilgrim, 2004). The Management Advisory Service (MAS) report (1989) attempted to set out these defining features.

The report identified three levels of psychological skills: level one involves the use of fundamental counselling skills; level two skills refers to the capacity to undertaking protocol-based interventions, such as manualised psychological therapies; and level three skills referred to a more flexible, comprehensive knowledge of psychological theories, which enables the development of tailored strategies for complex presentations (Huey & Britton, 2002; MAS, 1989). The report (MAS, 1989) concluded that clinical psychology is the only profession that operates at all three levels. While I feel that this ability may be unique, it is still somewhat lacking in providing clarity of the unique contribution; how does this give added value? It has been suggested that the profession's success in adopting various roles (working across all three levels) has created a perception that clinical psychologists do a little of everything, resulting in unrealistic expectations, further blurring of boundaries and a difficulty in pinpointing the direct value of the profession (DCP, 2007; Page & Stritzke, 2014).

To offer greater clarity and cohesiveness to the work of teams, it is important for clinical psychologists to share an established understanding of their professional identity in a way that is comprehensible to others. This may improve interdisciplinary and even multiagency working, which may be particularly important in settings where MDT working has been highlighted as particularly beneficial, such as in CAMHS. Due to the inconsistencies regarding the value of the profession, it may also be necessary for clinical psychologists to explicitly demonstrate the aspects of their professional identity that are unique and valuable to teams (DCP, 2007). But how do we do this when it appears that we have such difficulty articulating our identity to ourselves or each other?

My quest for answers

During clinical training, I battled with this question considerably. Whenever I asked those around me, both qualified and non-qualified psychologists, there was a distinct lack of clarity and confidence amongst the profession in defining a unique identity. This commenced a brief professional existential crisis for me. Who are we? What do we offer? Who am I supposed to be within all of this? What is the identity of a clinical psychologist, and what is *unique* about this? What differentiates what we offer from the contributions of other professions?

If you have asked yourself these types of questions (or if you are now, having read this), I hope it is good to know that you are not alone. But how do you go about answering such a difficult question?

Before you read on, I encourage you to take a moment to reflect on what you feel the professional identity of a clinical psychologist is to you. Perhaps make a note of what you feel your professional identity is. If you aren't qualified or in training yet, perhaps think about what you hope your identity will be – or should be.

Given my own confusion, my knowledge of the debates outlined earlier and the lack of reassurance I felt from my questioning of those around me, I thought it best to go searching for more answers; something I could use. Using individual semi-structured interviews, I completed a small-scale qualitative service evaluation with a group of clinical psychologists in CAMHS, seeking to explore their views regarding the unique identity and contribution of clinical psychologists to these teams (Simpson-Adkins, Hodge, & Gwilliam, 2015). All participants were qualified clinical psychologists working in CAMHS teams, with experience in terms of years since qualification ranging from one and a half to ten years.

The findings of this research proposed a model of the professional identity of clinical psychologists in CAMHS, which I have personally found helpful during my own professional development. I feel this is relatively transferable across different teams and settings in which clinical psychologists might work. A summary of the themes within this model are presented here, not as a demonstration of *the* identity of clinical psychology, but simply as a means of providing a springboard for your own reflection on the professional identity of the profession.

How did other clinical psychologists describe their identity?

The professional identity of clinical psychologists in CAMHS was seen as complex and multidimensional, and participants unsurprisingly found it difficult to describe this in a distinct way. Participants depicted a multiplicity of separate, yet complementary professional identities; some more explicit or frequently used than others. Specifically, they referred not just to being able, but also being actively willing to adapt roles and offer a flexible approach to personalising psychological approaches for young people and their families. This concept of willingness and enthusiasm, alongside the ability to adapt or perform different roles, distinguished their identity from that of other professionals. I feel that perhaps this demonstrates that it's not just what we do, it's how we do it.

It was agreed that each of the sub-identities clinical psychologists associated themselves with and the roles acted out within them can be found separately within other professions in CAMHS. However, only clinical psychologists were considered to encompass all of these identities and be capable, willing or expected to perform each or all of these identities. It was suggested that this multiplicity and flexibility of identities is what constitutes the professional identity and contribution of clinical psychology to these teams. The metaphor of a Swiss army knife was used to illustrate this idea.

The swiss army knife of CAMHS: a multiplicity of professional identities

The Swiss army knife has long been a trusted companion across the world, thanks to its versatility and integration of various handy tools. The description of clinical psychologists as being akin to Swiss army knives was felt to encapsulate the way in which participants related this multiplicity of identities as resembling a sense of multifunctionality; having multiple identities at one's disposal. All of the professional identities may not be needed all of the time, but the concept of having multiple tools enables one to perform multiple tasks, unlike a tool that is specifically designed for only a single task.

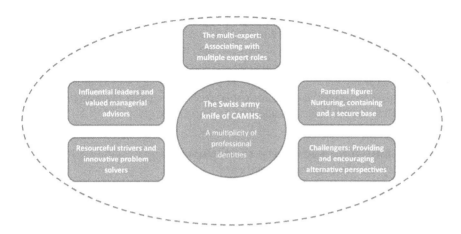

Figure 5.1 The adaptable nature of clinical psychologists in CAMHS

The multiple identities distinguished from analysis include these:

The multi-expert: associating with multiple expert roles. Participants described a variety of expert roles or activities which they either felt they were associated with or we are implicitly and explicitly requested to adopt within CAMHS. For instance, they described roles as expert therapists (in relation to direct work with children and their families), expert supervisors (helping colleagues overcome challenges or blocks), expert thinkers (providing thinking space and encouraging reflection within teams), expert researchers (conducting in-service and wider research, evaluation and audit projects), expert trainers and experts in understanding mental health and evidence-based practice guidelines.

A parental figure: providing nurturance, containment and a secure base for CAMHS teams. This identity encompasses the supportive, nurturing and emotionally containing identity of clinical psychologists in CAMHS teams. Although not formally requested or tasked to do so, almost all participants portrayed an unofficial responsibility to take on this metaphorical parenting role and provide a secure base; to be available to other members of the team, to provide care, support and containment, particularly in times of stress, and to provide nurturance via skill development, particularly through modelling and encouragement.

The challengers: providing and encouraging alternative perspectives. Many of the participants explained that a unique skill of clinical psychologists is the ability to integrate and share multiple perspectives, which encourages reflection on approaches taken within a team; often offering healthy challenge to dominant discourses and encouraging inclusive practice.

Resourceful strivers and innovative problem solvers. Clinical psychologists identified themselves as highly driven, innovative problem solvers that seek out and facilitate team and individual development, while bringing in valuable additional resources to the perceived benefit of the team.

Influential leaders and managerial advisors. Participants portrayed an identity of being actively sought out to provide what is often unofficial leadership and managerial or strategic guidance. Participants felt well trained and willing to take on such leadership responsibility.

Could this be an identity that causes as many problems as it solves?

The analysis revealed that the participants felt that clinical psychologists were still misunderstood within their CAMHS teams, and there was a seemingly unspoken pressure from the teams for psychologists to prove their worth. Consequently, and without necessarily being requested to do so, participants described feeling pulled into frequently switching between these multiple sub-identities in order to respond to constantly incoming and evolving service pressures; thus demonstrating their value to the team. However, as a result of this desire to remain adaptable in response to the contextual demands of a service, it appears that the professional identity remains in a constant state of flux; shifting between the different sub-identities functioning within the principal Swiss army knife identity. Therefore, this act seems to actually maintain the lack of role clarity for other professions and thus perpetuate, rather than relieve (as intended), the perceived threat of unrecognised value.

Food for thought

The proposed unique strength of the profession, the characteristically adaptable Swiss army knife, was also perceived by those within the profession as a potential frailty, which may even one day jeopardise the future of the profession. However, I do not personally feel that the willingness or ability to be responsive to demand is a weakness. Perhaps it is our lack of explicit ownership and ability to highlight this strength that threatens the value of the profession.

Helping to develop this model has been useful for me during my training and in the early stages of my career in clinical psychology. It has encouraged me not only to contemplate my developing professional identity, but also the sub-identities that I feel represent my practice – many of which actually feel quite similar to those described earlier. I feel that it is key for those of us within, entering or considering entry into the profession to continue giving careful thought to the professional identity of clinical psychology, both individually and as a collective. There is also a desperate need to make our professional identity, whatever this may be, more explicitly understood by colleagues, stakeholders and commissioners. A clear personal and collective understanding can inform and influence the contextual demands placed on the profession, at public, service and organisational levels.

If you made a note of your thoughts on professional identity earlier, perhaps it might be helpful to look back at this now and consider whether or not connects with the model described. What sub-identities would make up your Swiss army knife? It might also be helpful to reflect on how you could explicitly communicate your ideas on the professional identity of a clinical psychologist with your colleagues, both within and outside of the profession. Would this be different to how you would explain this to someone using a service you were working in?

Conclusion

This chapter proposes a model of the professional identity of clinical psychologists in CAMHS teams. The model reflects the complexity and multidimensional nature of the role. The model may offer clinical psychologists a pragmatic way of articulating their professional identity; though this is intended only as a starting point, and we would encourage adaptation to local service context. This model may facilitate personal and intra-professional reflection regarding the identity of clinical psychology, which may help to reduce the sense of threat and enhance work-related self-esteem (Hogg & Terry, 2001). By considering ways to develop a sense of confident ownership of our individual and collective strengths, the profession will be in a better position to solidify and capitalise on knowledge and expertise.

This may also provide a platform for trainee, assistant and aspiring clinical psychologists to reflect on the development of their professional identity. During my career so far as a clinical psychologist, I feel that the Swiss army knife metaphor and the sub-identities contained within it are somewhat representative of how it feels personally to work in a variety of team settings. It has also helped me to have conversations with other professions about who we are as a group, and who I am within this. I hope that this chapter will encourage you to reflect on your own identity and inspire you to share that identity with others.

Suggested further reading

Cheshire, K., & Pilgrim, D. (2004). *A short introduction to clinical psychology*. London: SAGE Publications Ltd.

References

British Psychological Society. (2007). *Leading psychological services: A report by the Division of Clinical Psychology*. Leicester: British Psychological Society.
Cheshire, K., & Pilgrim, D. (2004). *A short introduction to clinical psychology*. London: SAGE Publications Ltd.
Christofides, S., Johnstone, L., & Musa, M. (2012). 'Chipping in': Clinical psychologists' descriptions of their use of formulation in multidisciplinary team working. *Psychology*

and Psychotherapy: Theory, Research & Practice, 85(4), 424–435. doi:10.1111/j.2044-8341.2011.02041.x

Department of Health. (2003). *Agenda for change: Proposed agreement.* London: Department of Health. Retrieved from www.dhsspsni.gov.uk/scu-agendachange-proposed agreement.pdf

Department of Health. (2004). *National service framework for children, young people and maternity services: The mental health and psychological well-being of children and young people.* Retrieved from www.gov.uk/government/uploads/system/uploads/attachment_data/file/199959/National_Service_Framework_for_Children_Young_Peo ple_and_Maternity_Services_-_The_Mental_Health__and_Psychological_Well-being_ of_Children_and_Young_People.pdf

Division of Clinical Psychology (DCP). (2007). *Understanding customer needs of clinical psychology services.* London: Mental Health Strategies. Retrieved from http:// dcp.bps.org.uk/document-download-area/document-download$.cfm?file_uuid=C632 2119-1143-DFD0-7E93-B00EB8C50F8F

Hogg, M. A., & Terry, D. J. (2001). Social identity theory and organizational processes. In M. A. Hogg & D. J. Terry (Eds.), *Social identity processes in organizational contexts* (pp. 1–12). Philadelphia, PA: Psychology Press.

Huey, D. A., & Britton, P. G. (2002). A portrait of clinical psychology. *Journal of Interprofessional Care, 16*(1), 69–78. doi:10.1080/13561820220104186

Kutash, K., Acri, M., Pollock, M., Armusewicz, K., Olin, S. S., & Hoagwood, K. E. (2014). Quality indicators for multidisciplinary team functioning in community-based children's mental health services. *Administration and Policy in Mental Health, 41*(1), 55–68. doi:10.1007/s10488-013-0508-2

Lancaster, S., & Smith, D. I. (2002). What's in a name? The identity of clinical psychology as a specialty. *Australian Psychologist, 37*(1), 48–51. doi:10.1080/00050060210001 706666

Management Advisory Service (MAS). (1989). *Review of clinical psychology services: Activities and possible models.* Retrieved from www.mas.org.uk/uploads/articles/MAS %20Review%201989.pdf

Miller, C., & Ahmad, Y. (2000). Collaboration and partnership: An effective response to complexity and fragmentation or solution built on sand? *International Journal of Sociology and Social Policy, 20*(5–6), 1–38. doi:10.1108/01443330010789151

Page, A. C., & Stritzke, W. G. (2014). *Clinical psychology for trainees.* Cambridge, UK: Cambridge University Press.

Salmon, G. (2004). Multi-agency collaboration: The challenges for CAMHS. *Child and Adolescent Mental Health, 9*(4), 156–161. doi: 10.1111/j.1475-3588.2004.00099.x

Simpson-Adkins, G., Hodge, S., & Gwilliam, P. (2015). *Exploring the views of clinical psychologists regarding the unique identity and contribution of clinical psychology in CAMHS services: A qualitative analysis.* (Unpublished manuscript).

Chapter 6

Thinking about risk

Developing my identity as a clinical psychologist through experiences of risk assessment and management

Bethan Roberts

Summary points

- Trainee clinical psychologists undergo significant development in their own competence and professional identity throughout training. Learning to manage risk is a key part of this development.
- Professional development relates to the ability to manage risk, and this evolves over time and through experience.
- Both individual and wider systemic factors are vital to consider, as is the importance of good supervision and support in facilitating learning and development.

This chapter focuses on one specific aspect of the training process – learning how to assess and manage *risk*. For the purposes of this chapter, risk refers to the likelihood of a person engaging in a specific risk behaviour, such as harm to self or others. When discussing risk, the process of *risk assessment* (the collection of information to determine the likelihood of harm occurring) and *risk management* (the implementation of a set of strategies or ideas aimed at reducing the likelihood of risk occurring) are often considered. The concept of risk is central to the role of clinical psychologists, who may increasingly be responsible for this assessment and management within clinical services (British Psychological Society [BPS], 2006). Consequently, learning to manage risk is a key part of clinical psychology training, and can elicit elevated levels of anxiety and concern. Managing risk encompasses a range of skills and actions and often depends on a combination of structured assessments alongside clinical judgement (Borum, 1996).

Building my confidence in managing risk was a process which happened alongside the development of my identity as a competent clinical psychologist. As my identity as a practitioner developed, so did my ability to rely on my professional judgement in relation to identifying and managing risk issues. To demonstrate my developing understanding of identity and of risk throughout the training process I will share some specific examples which symbolise these changes. I will also explore the context in which this learning took place.

To become qualified, trainee clinical psychologists must demonstrate competence and understanding across several areas (Health and Care Professions Council [HCPC], 2009b). In addition to gaining specific knowledge to inform practice within a diverse range of settings and specialities, clinical psychology training programmes also aim to develop trainee's abilities to engage critically with existing evidence, and to work as reflective practitioners (BPS, 2010).

The acquisition of new skills influences the way in which trainees perceive themselves as professional practitioners, with evidence suggesting that an individual's professional identity must adapt to integrate new information (Bruss & Kopala, 1993; Ibarra, 1999). Professional identity refers to (1) the way in which we see ourselves as professional practitioners, (2) the way in which we present ourselves professionally to others and (3) the way in which others perceive us as professionals (Adams, Hean, Sturgis, & Clark, 2006). A well-developed professional identity is linked to self-efficacy, competence and decision-making (Davis et al., 2003; Ibarra, 1999).

Research suggests that an individual's self-perceived identity can also specifically influence the way in which he/she understands and responds to clinical risk, and with the way in which an individual identifies within a professional group mediating his/her clinical decisions (Ibarra, 1999). Thinking about risk was strongly related to my own developing professional identity as a clinical psychologist. Reflecting on this process helped me to notice changes in my relationships with other professionals, my sense of autonomy and my level of initiative.

Several models have attempted to conceptualise the process of professional development during training (e.g., Rønnestad & Skovholt, 2003; Stoltenberg, 1998). The Rønnestad and Skovholt model (2003) focuses not only on development during training but also recognises that therapist development continues throughout the lifespan. Six phases of development are described: the lay helper, the beginning student, the advanced student, the novice professional, the experienced professional and the senior professional. The model also emphasises the extent that an individual experiences and professional relationships interact to influence professional development. I plan to consider my own professional development in relation to these stages and will reflect on what has helped to inform and influence this development.

Experimenting through observing role models

My first placement was in a Child and Adolescent Mental Health Service in the NHS. In an early session with a 12-year-old service user, Vince (pseudonyms used throughout), he disclosed that in the past he had experienced thoughts about ending his life. I was able to ask him some exploratory questions around this and tried to contain his anxiety about telling me. I then asked him to wait with his mother while I spoke to my supervisor about planning a course of action.

My supervisor and I reflected on this experience and I was able to recognise that although I had appeared confident in my responses, internally I was anxious and had felt that I needed to follow the advice they gave me without question. In response to this uncertainty I ensured that I become more familiar with the service policy around risk management and read BPS guidelines around managing and formulating risks for psychologists (BPS, 2006).

For me, this approach demonstrates that as a practitioner I was heavily dependent on guidance from others and lacked the confidence to make decisions independently. My focus was on developing practical skills and knowledge at the expense of critical thinking. The reliance on others and lack of confidence present here suggest that I was acting as a *beginning student* (Rønnestad & Skovholt, 2003). At this stage, an individual's sense of self has not been clearly established. The process of adapting the self to a new professional role includes observation and imitation of role models in the field (Ibarra, 1999).

I believe that this model fits with my approach here. Although I acted correctly and professionally in my behaviour, I did so through relying on my supervisor as a role model. To internalise this sense of professional belonging, Ibarra (1999) suggests that we must first portray a credible image to others in the hope that their perception of us as competent will impact on our own self-perception. In order to portray a credible image, I needed to rely on the relative safety of what my supervisor would do. Externally I was able to appear competent, yet this sense of agency was not internalised.

Belonging to a professional group

My adult placement was within an adult psychological therapies service. This service formed part of the local community mental health team and so offered therapeutic input to individuals who would often describe a complex history of mental health difficulties. I worked with Mike, a 49-year-old male experiencing chronic low mood who would regularly talk about wanting to end his life. I spoke to Mike's social worker, Simon, on several occasions during our time working together to address this risk of suicide. I found this process challenging as Simon would often perceive the risk as less urgent than I did. I spent time thinking about the part that risk might play in Simon's job role, and about his level of experience. This helped me to understand why it was likely that Simon would view risk from a different perspective to myself.

Simon was an experienced social worker within a community mental health team which frequently managed elevated levels of risk, whereas I was at the time a first-year trainee clinical psychologist with limited experience in this area. Evidence suggests that multiple factors mediate our responses to risks, amongst these are environmental context and frequency of exposure to high-risk situations (Borum, 1996). In this case our previous experiences could have influenced our assessment of Mike's risk. Amalberti, Auroy, Barach and Berwick (2005) report that healthcare professionals will often take on the characteristics of a particular professional group and will perceive themselves as belonging to that group. It has been suggested that professional groups vary in their boundaries of what is deemed acceptable when managing risk and that the more an individual identifies with a group the more visible these differences will become (McDonald et al., 2005).

Thinking about these differences in our exposure to risk and in our priorities as professionals aided me in being able to have more open communication with Simon. Separating the aspects of the situation that were real and current and what aspects might be better explained by my anxiety gave me confidence in being able to reassert my own views and in starting to believe that I did have a valid perspective which deserved a voice. As a result, Simon and I were able to work closely together to develop a comprehensive risk management strategy. We were able to ensure that Mike had access to sources of support during periods of crisis and that key indicators that his mood was deteriorating were clearly identified.

This case proved a starting point in me being able to be aware of my own position and opinion, rather than automatically following the advice of others more senior to me. It also supported me in further expanding my view of risk from being something objective and quantifiable to being at least partially dependent on the background, experience and outlook of the person viewing it. Rønnestad and Skovholt (2003) might recognise that I was beginning to exhibit behaviour in keeping with the *advanced students/interns* stage of development, which is characterised by beginning to assert one's own views, rather than accepting the opinions of others unquestioningly (Rønnestad & Skovholt, 2003).

Organisational factors

My final six-month core placement was within a community learning disabilities team, and I then stayed in this team for a further nine months as a specialist placement. The team employed a person-centred and human rights–based approach to risk management. I was given opportunities to support with service development alongside my clinical work. The values and ideals of this team were similar to those that I recognise within myself, which helped me to think about the role of organisational set-up in the way in which we identify as professionals. This focus on contextual issues suggests that I was well established within the *advanced students/interns* stage of development (Rønnestad & Skovholt, 2003), as I continued to be able to confront conflicts between my own values and those of others.

Within this placement I was involved in developing and contributing to some projects exploring the application of a human rights–based approach to working with risk. This approach focuses on the importance of service user involvement and co-production, and ensures that any decisions around risk are made in a person-centred way, representing the least-restrictive option available (Greenhill & Whitehead, 2010). Through contributing to this project, I was able to reflect on my own approach to risk, and on the difficulties that clinicians experience in balancing different responsibilities. On one hand we have a duty of care to service users – meaning that we have a responsibility to take reasonable care to ensure that our actions or inactions do not cause injury or harm to others. However, *dignity of risk* refers to the freedom which individuals should have to make decisions and choices which may expose them to risks (Perske, 1972). I noticed that in some of my previous experience I was perhaps placing too much emphasis on my own duty of care without being able to consider the rights and opinions of the service users I was working with (Department of Health, 2001, 2007).

Throughout my time on the placement, I made time in supervision to discuss my own anxieties around managing risk, and to think about how to ensure that the person-centred values so central to my way of working were also present when considering risk. One way in which I did this was through using human rights–based risk assessment tools (Whitehead, Carney, & Greenhill, 2011). These are tools which were developed with a person-centred collaborative approach in mind and helped me to ensure that my focus remained in the right place, while still providing me with a tool to assess risk appropriately and to way to justify some of my decisions.

Sharing responsibility around risk

Nicholson (1984) suggests that when an individual has transitioned into a new work role it brings about changes to him/her as a person, to his/her role or to both. While I was able to demonstrate progress throughout training I was also mindful of research suggesting that it is not until an individual leaves the safety of a student perspective and takes on a qualified role that his/her burgeoning professional identity is truly challenged and reformed (Ibarra, 1999). This idea is complemented by necessity to continue to seek opportunities for professional development in order to meet the requirements of registration with the Health and Care Professions Council (HCPC, 2009a). Rønnestad and Skovholt (2003) also recognised the extent to which post-training experiences shape professional identity, with three of their six identified phases applying only to qualified professionals.

One area in which I have noticed considerable change is in my ability to tolerate the possibility of risk in others. I have strived to find a balance between duty of care and dignity of risk approaches, ensuring that service users can safely live their lives in a way where they are minimally restricted by services. My work within learning disability services has made me aware of the extent to which services attempt to manage the risk of service users and will often inadvertently pathologise behaviour which may be tolerated outside of services. For example, when working with young service users who enjoy nights out and consuming alcohol, I am aware that this is behaviour which is common for many people. However within services, it might lead to elevated levels of concern and to attempts to limit or control alcohol use. Through using opportunities to encourage staff teams to share their concerns, and through speaking with service users about their opinions and desires it is often possible to achieve a compromise where service users can take responsibility for their own risks and where services feel well equipped to support this. Rønnestad and Skovholt (2003) might recognise that I am moving through the *novice professional* stage, which can last for several years and is characterised by self-exploration, reflection and development of the self as an autonomous professional.

Conclusion

Through reflecting on my own development I have been able to observe a growing confidence and changing attitude towards risk management. During early placements, I was often reliant on the opinions of others to inform my decisions and saw it as my sole responsibility to manage and assess risk issues which arose.

While I continue to hold clinical responsibility for my decisions, I have become increasingly comfortable with facilitating open and honest conversations with service users exploring their own confidence in managing their risks. I have been able to develop plans which recognise the presence of risk but also empower the individual to feel able to manage this risk rather than trying to remove it from him/her. This change in practice has developed from an increased confidence in my own ability, alongside an increased recognition of myself as someone belonging to a professional group for whom managing and working with risk in a person-centred way is crucial.

Suggested further reading

British Psychological Society. (2006). *Risk assessment and management.* Leicester: The British Psychological Society.

Greenhill, B., & Whitehead, R. (2010). Promoting service user inclusion in risk assessment and management: A pilot project developing a human rights-based approach. *British Journal of Learning Disabilities, 39,* 277–283. doi:10.1111/j.1468-3156.2010.00664.x

Rønnestad, M. H., & Skovholt, T. M. (2003). The journey of the counselor and therapist: Research findings and perspectives on professional development. *Journal of Career Development, 30*(1), 5–44. doi:10.1023/A:1025173508081

Whittington, R., & Logan, C. (2011). *Self-harm and violence: Towards best practice in managing risk in mental health services.* Chichester: Wiley-Blackwell.

References

Adams, K., Hean, S., Sturgis, P., & Clark, J. M. (2006). Investigating the factors influencing professional identity of first-year health and social care students. *Learning in Health and Social Care, 5*(2), 55–68. doi:10.1111/j.1473-6861.2006.00119.x

Amalberti, R., Auroy, Y., Barach, P., & Berwick, D. M. (2005). Five system barriers to achieving ultrasafe health care. *Annals of Internal Medicine, 142,* 756–764. doi:10.7326/0003-4819-142-9-200505030-00012

Borum, R. (1996). Improving the clinical practice of violence risk assessment: Technology, guidelines, and training. *American Psychologist, 51*(9), 945–956. doi:10.1037/0003-066X.51.9.945

British Psychological Society. (2006). *Risk assessment and management.* Leicester: The British Psychological Society.

British Psychological Society. (2010). *Accreditation through partnership handbook: Guidance for clinical programmes.* Leicester: The British Psychological Society.

Bruss, K. V., & Kopala, M. (1993). Graduate school training in psychology: Its impact upon the development of professional identity. *Psychotherapy: Theory, Research, Practice, Training, 30*(4), 685–691. doi:10.1037/0033-3204.30.4.685

Davis, R. E., Dolan, G., Thomas, S., Atwell, C., Mead, D., Nehammer, S., . . . Elwyn, G. (2003). Exploring doctor and patient views about risk communication and shared decision-making in the consultation. *Health Expectations, 6*(3), 198–207. doi:10.1046/j.1369-6513.2003.00235.x

Department of Health. (2001). *Valuing people: A new strategy for learning disability for the 21st century: Implementation.* London: Department of Health.

Department of Health. (2007). *Human rights in healthcare – A framework for local action.* London: Department of Health.

Greenhill, B., & Whitehead, R. (2010). Promoting service user inclusion in risk assessment and management: A pilot project developing a human rights-based approach. *British Journal of Learning Disabilities, 39,* 277–283.

Health and Care Professions Council. (2009a). *Standards of proficiency – Practitioner psychologists.* London: HCPC.

Health and Care Professions Council. (2009b). *Standards of education and training – Practitioner psychologists.* London: HCPC.

Ibarra, H. (1999). Provisional selves: Experimenting with image and identity in professional adaptation. *Administrative Science Quarterly, 44*(4), 764–791. doi:10.2307/2667055

McDonald, R., Waring, J., Harrison, S., Boaden, R., Walshe, K., & Parker, D. (2005). *An ethnographic study of threats to patient safety in the operating theatre. Final report of a study funded by the Patient Safety Research Programme.* Retrieved from www.haps.bham.ac.uk/publichealth/psrp/documents/PS008_Final_Report_Harrison.pdf

Nicholson, N. (1984). A theory of work role transitions. *Administrative Science Quarterly, 29,* 172–191. doi:10.2307/2393172

Perske, R. (1972). The dignity of risk and the mentally retarded. *Mental Retardation, 10*(1), 24–27.

Rønnestad, M. H., & Skovholt, T. M. (2003). The journey of the counselor and therapist: Research findings and perspectives on professional development. *Journal of Career Development, 30*(1), 5–44. doi:10.1023/A:1025173508081

Stoltenberg, C. D. (1998). A social cognitive – And developmental – Model of counselor training. *The Counseling Psychologist, 26,* 317–323. doi:10.1177/0011000098262007

Whitehead, R., Carney, G., & Greenhill, B. (2011). Encouraging positive risk management: Supporting decisions by people with learning disabilities using a human rights-based approach. In R. Whittington & C. Logan (Eds.), *Self-harm and violence: Towards best practice in managing risk in mental health services* (pp. 215–236). Chichester: Wiley-Blackwell.

Chapter 7

Professional issues in neuropsychological assessment

Lindsay Prescott, John Timney and Thomas Rozwaha

Summary points

- Neuropsychological assessment is a core competency for clinical psychologists and forms part of their unique professional identity and value to physical and mental health services.
- These skills are vital to ensure that neuropsychological issues are considered within clinical practice, both when working with an individual and when working as part of a multidisciplinary team.
- The clinical psychologist must utilise their unique skill set to address and overcome professional issues regarding neuropsychological assessment.

Clinical neuropsychology is the application of a scientific understanding to the relationship between the brain and a person's cognitive, emotional and behavioural functioning within an applied clinical context (British Psychological Society [BPS], 2012b). The use of specific standardised tests within neuropsychological assessment can provide a measurement of various cognitive functions, including attention, memory, language, visual and executive skills. Clinical psychologists utilise neuropsychological assessment across a wide range of services, most commonly in acute hospital settings, brain injury services, dementia/memory assessment services, educational settings and learning disability services (BPS, 2012b). Neuropsychological assessments might be used in these contexts to understand the impact of an acquired brain injury (e.g., stroke, traumatic brain injury), assess changes in cognitive functioning over time to monitor progressing dementia, explore the cognitive strengths and difficulties of a child struggling at school or establish an individual's overall intellectual ability and needs.

Within healthcare services, clinical psychologists are often regarded as experts in hypothesis-driven neuropsychological and cognitive assessment, and professional guidance states that in-depth neuropsychological assessment should involve a qualified clinical psychologist (BPS, 2012b). Clinical psychologists are trained to have a baseline level of expertise in neuropsychological assessment and formulation, fulfilling core competencies as part of doctorate training. Following this, some clinical psychologists also go on to complete additional qualification (composed of theoretical and clinical work) to join a specialist register of clinical neuropsychologists (Collerton & Domone, 2014).

Neuropsychological assessment is a broad and complex area. Experiencing ethical and professional dilemmas when providing neuropsychological assessment in practice has helped to shape our professional identities within the context of clinical psychology. We will reflect on some of these experiences over the chapter.

Inter-disciplinary working

Increasingly, clinical psychologists are employed to work within multidisciplinary teams (MDTs), working collaboratively with other professional disciplines such as psychiatry, occupational therapy, speech and language therapy and nursing. While MDT working is considered an advancement in providing integrated patient care, establishing a unique professional identity can be difficult, particularly within medical environments.

Despite neuropsychological assessment being a core competency of clinical psychologists, other professional disciplines (such as occupational therapy or speech and language therapy) also utilise some cognitive assessment tools. These vary in complexity, from short bedside cognitive screening tools, such as the Mini Mental State Examination (MMSE; Folstein, Folstein, & McHugh, 1975), to more specific assessments such as the Rivermead Behavioural Memory test (Wilson, Cockburn, & Baddeley,1985).

Cognitive assessment tools like these can be helpful in providing a snapshot of a person's current difficulties, or to understand his/her ability in relation to one specific area of functioning. However, it is important to distinguish these from comprehensive neuropsychological assessments, generally conducted by a clinical psychologist or clinical neuropsychologist. Neuropsychological assessment is generally broad in scope, seeking to understand more complex presentations where a more intricate and thorough understanding of functioning across a range of areas is required. However, other professionals in the MDT can also undergo specialist training to conduct some assessment tools often utilised by clinical psychologists – so what is our unique role in the team?

As our experience has grown, our definition of neuropsychological assessment from the perspective of a clinical psychologist has become broader. Our earlier understandings of neuropsychological assessment perhaps reflected a common misperception: that testing is about delivering a battery of tests, adhering to standardisations during administration and calculating the scores using a manual which are compared to standardised samples, in order to decipher which particular cognitive areas reflect strengths or weaknesses for our client. However, through a combination of clinical supervision and the development of wider psychological formulation skills, we have become aware of the greater complexities involved in a comprehensive neuropsychological assessment. This includes assessment preparation (i.e., choosing an appropriate set of tests which help to test hypotheses) and considering qualitative observations during testing, to holistic interpretation of the results as part of a formulation and communicating feedback to different audiences, either verbally or via a written report.

Assessment requires an integration of test results with observations of qualitative information (e.g., level of distraction, motivation, engagement) and contextual awareness (e.g., prior education, socioeconomic status, cultural background), within a framework that allows for an understanding of the cognitive, social, emotional, psychological and systemic aspects that may be contributing to a person's functioning in a given situation. As such, understanding a person's neuropsychological strengths and difficulties requires a holistic *formulation* of the interplay between each of these aspects, applying theory to practice, and interpreting test observations in the real-world context. Skills in formulation have been described as a defining competency of all applied psychologists, and understanding neuropsychological test results in the context of the individual is often what can define the professional identity of a clinical psychologist within a multidisciplinary team (BPS, 2011b).

Potential tensions can arise between professionals when there are misunderstandings about the role of clinical psychologists in relation to neuropsychological assessment. We have seen polarised examples of such tensions in our experiences, from the misconception that a comprehensive neuropsychological assessment is appropriate for all clients, to the lack of understanding of why a neuropsychological assessment by a clinical psychologist would be helpful. This may occur if, for example, a cognitive screening test has already been completed and the score (in relation to the pre-determined cut off scores) is accepted at face value without consideration of wider factors which might affect the validity of the results. Situations such as these can cause disagreement and disharmony with a team and negatively impact on patient care.

In one such example of a situation which might cause disagreement within a team around the role of psychology, one of the authors of this chapter was working on an adult mental health ward when he/she was asked by the MDT to conduct a neuropsychological assessment on a gentleman who presented with difficulty regulating strong emotions, self-harming behaviour and suspected learning difficulties. This client had never been formally diagnosed with a learning disability, despite it being repeatedly mentioned by healthcare professionals over the 15 years that he had been known to services. One of the most challenging aspects of working with this client was that he believed others thought of him as "stupid", which was identified as a trigger for several risk-taking behaviours. He was unable to read but could reason well verbally.

Following supervision with a qualified clinical psychologist, it was agreed that conducting a formal assessment would not be in the man's best interests as it would likely only strengthen his belief that others thought of him as stupid. It was also recognised that the assessment would not grant him any greater access to care than was currently available to him. In lieu of an assessment, we worked with the gentleman and co-constructed a more holistic support plan, which helped him to feel that he was valued on the ward and facilitated the professionals working with him to feel confident in supporting him effectively. In this situation, it was particularly important to feed back the rationale for not conducting a neuropsychological assessment to the team to support their understanding of this decision and avoid inter-disciplinary issues.

Clinical psychologists hold many non-clinical roles within services, including clinical leadership, training and education of other professions within a team (BPS, 2012a). Given clinical psychologist's specialist knowledge and training in neuropsychological theory and testing, they are in a unique position to teach, supervise and provide consultation in line with the competencies expected of all practitioner psychologists (Collerton & Domone, 2014; Health and Care Professions Council, 2015). This is easier said than done, but nevertheless this important approach to dealing with these issues and improving the effectiveness of MDT working is increasingly apparent as we progress in our careers. The reciprocal relationship between our growing confidence in understanding our own role as a clinical psychologist, and the experiences of dealing with the professional challenges described earlier, has helped to shape our current professional identity when working in this context.

Dissemination of results

Clinical psychologists conduct holistic and often complex interpretations of a person's neuropsychological strengths and difficulties. A key role of a clinical psychologist is to then decide how best to feedback the results to the client or his/her family and often to other professionals involved in his/her care.

In our experience, individual clinical psychologists and the services in which they work can vary regarding their preferred method of communicating the results of neuropsychological assessment. Across earlier experiences of writing up neuropsychological assessment results, one author found it increasingly frustrating after spending much time and effort writing up lengthy and detailed reports (as was common practice within the service), for other professionals to request executive summaries or main points of the report. Even though these requests for simplified, jargon-free versions were perfectly reasonable, we wonder whether part of the desire to produce such comprehensive reports reflected a desire of clinical psychologists to form a unique and valued professional identity, demonstrating the complexity and expertise of neuropsychological assessment to others. Although it is common within some services for neuropsychological assessment results to be formally written into a report, we have become increasingly mindful of the appropriateness of sharing complex results and the need for considering the purpose of the report and the needs of the target audience.

As it is likely that clients will be undergoing assessment because there are identified or suspected cognitive difficulties due to their neurological condition, compensations by the clinical psychologist are often needed in the method of feedback. Ensuring accessibility for the client and adaptations to suit his/her individual strengths and weaknesses, as found in the assessment results, are key considerations. Importantly, the language used in any verbal feedback to the client (as well as in the final clinical report) must hold the client's level of comprehension in mind, as complex neuropsychological interpretations may distance and disempower a client, damaging the therapeutic relationship.

One example of individually adapting the feedback of neuropsychological assessment results comes from one author's recent experience of working with a 10-year-old girl who was struggling at school following a history of trauma and anxiety. To aid her understanding, carefully chosen findings were presented to the girl in simple language and in short bullet points, each linking to a real-life example of how this related to her at school and home. Information was presented on a single page and in three parts (strengths, struggles and what can help), each forming part of a butterfly image. This helped to engage the client and make the delivery of results less anxiety-provoking. A supplementary report was provided to her parents to support their understanding of the interaction between their daughter's cognitive ability and emotional functioning, based on a holistic formulation of her presenting difficulties.

Reflecting on our experiences of feeding back test results to individuals who have varying ability levels and neuropsychological impairment, there are now three questions that we keep in mind before embarking on direct client feedback:

(1) What are the most important pieces of information to communicate?
(2) What are the most useful pieces of information for them to know?
(3) How will I present the information to the client in a way that will support him/her to best understand and remember it?

While a temptation exists to limit direct client feedback if there are concerns relating to his/her level of comprehension, the ethical expectation for openness with a client means that feedback should be given whenever possible (BPS, 2017). Evidence suggests that directly communicating information relating to cognitive difficulties the client may be experiencing improved treatment outcomes and independence (Pegg et al., 2005).

The power imbalance experienced between the clinical psychologist and his/her client must also be considered when giving neuropsychological assessment feedback. The interpretation of test results can have an impact on care decisions, long-term service provision and client wellbeing (Camp, Skrajner, Lee, & Judge, 2010; Russo, Bush, & Rasin-Waters, 2013). A client's experience of hearing his/her test results, and the understanding he/she takes away from a feedback session, can strongly influence his/her developing sense of identity, self-esteem and emotional wellbeing – which may be changing in response to his/her health condition or diagnosis. A study aiming to understand the level of information that healthy volunteers could remember following feedback of neuropsychological test results showed that retention levels of key facts can be significantly lower than expected (Bennett-Levy, Klein-Boonschate, Batchelor, McCarter, & Walton, 1994).

The need to hold the person at the centre of any conversation surrounding potential diagnoses, and the responsibility to act as an advocate for a client, is a core part of our professional identity in these clinical situations. However, this can create ethical and professional issues, particularly in cases where clients might lack insight and awareness into their difficulties and at times, actively disagree with the results of neuropsychological assessment. In such cases, it can be useful to consider and draw on other psychological theories and models, such as self-awareness and emergent awareness to further understand and support clients and inform appropriate treatment plans (FitzGerald et al., 2017; Robertson & Schmitter-Edgecombe, 2015). We have come to realise that the ability to draw on and synthesise a range of psychological theories and models is another defining skill of clinical psychologists, allowing us to further develop a professional identity within neuropsychological contexts.

Training and competence in neuropsychological assessment

Cognitive testing (as part of a wider neuropsychological assessment) is often carried out by assistant psychologists and trainee clinical psychologists, who are not yet qualified and therefore cannot be assumed (or expected) to hold the same knowledge base as a qualified clinical psychologist. As a non-qualified individual conducting testing, close collaboration with and supervision from an appropriately trained clinical psychologist is clinically essential (BPS, 2011a). The BPS recommends at least two hours per week (pro rata) of supervision for assistant psychologists and one hour for trainee clinical psychologists by qualified practitioner psychologists (BPS, 2007, 2010); this should focus on helping ensure that the supervisee has the skill to provide high quality assessment, alongside discussion of wider contextual factors which might help make sense of the performance scores within a neuropsychological formulation.

Ongoing and high-quality supervision is also important post-qualification. All clinical psychologists are trained to meet core competencies in neuropsychological assessment and formulation. However, there can be great variability in clinical psychologist's experience in neuropsychological assessment both during training and post-qualification. Beyond training, it is the responsibility of individual clinical psychologists to ensure that they remain competent in these areas throughout qualified life, and maintain a critical stance towards the neuropsychological assessment tools that they use. For example, clinical psychologists should be aware of the normative sample used by test developers and be mindful that it may not be particularly relevant to the individual needs or context of the person they are working with; meaning that any conclusions drawn from cut off scores or norms may lack validity.

However, as neuropsychological assessment is a fast-moving field, and testing materials are frequently updated and altered, this is not always easy, particularly in services where neuropsychological assessment is not routinely offered. Clinical psychologists who work in settings where neuropsychological assessment is not a routine part of the work (e.g., mental health services) may not develop their confidence and competence post-qualification, leading to factors such as potential cognitive impairment being overlooked in the course of their clinical work. For example, would repeatedly missed appointments be interpreted as a sign of poor engagement, or a potential problem with memory secondary to an undiagnosed progressive neurological condition? Would impulsive behaviours be interpreted as a sign of emotional dysregulation, or an impairment in executive functioning skills in inhibiting behaviours due to a previous traumatic brain injury?

Neuropsychological issues are important to consider in all of the people we work with. Across any clinical setting, psychologists must be aware of their current competence in neuropsychological assessment, seeking supervision, additional training and support where needed. The combination of having the opportunity to conduct neuropsychological assessments in addition to regular supervision to understand and interpret results, has been instrumental in supporting the development of our professional identity as clinical psychologists within a neuropsychological context to date. We suspect that this journey will continue post-qualification and throughout our careers as clinical psychologists.

Conclusion

Clinical psychologists have a unique role within the MDT when performing neuropsychological assessment, combining their knowledge of neuropsychological processes and functioning with their skills in the holistic formulation of an individual within a specific context. Communicating this unique approach to neuropsychological assessment within inter-disciplinary teams can be difficult, and we have learned that the use of meaningful training and education alongside clinical and leadership skills is useful within this context when developing a professional identity as a clinical psychologist.

Providing an accessible and empowering interpretation of neuropsychological assessment results is important when feeding back the assessment results to clients, ensuring the information is meaningful to both clients and other professionals, with careful consideration given to how such feedback can support psychological wellbeing, self-identity and self-esteem. Clinical psychologists should also be aware of the importance of their confidence and competence in neuropsychological assessment and formulation, whatever their area of expertise or practice. They should be pro-active in supporting their own ongoing learning during and following qualification, to avoid overlooking neuropsychological issues and to help ensure that the needs of clients and MDTs are met in an integrated manner.

Suggested further reading

Hebben, N., & Milberg, W. (2009). *Essentials of neuropsychological assessment*. New Jersey: Wiley.

Postal, K., & Armstrong, K. (2013). *Feedback that sticks: The art of effectively communicating neuropsychological assessment results.* New York, NY: Oxford University Press.

Schoenberg, M. R., & Scott, J. G. (2011). *The little black book of neuropsychology: A syndrome-based approach.* New York, NY: Springer.

References

Bennett-Levy, J., Klein-Boonschate, M. A., Batchelor, J., McCarter, R., & Walton, N. (1994). Encounters with Anna Thompson: The consumer's experience of neuropsychological assessment. *Clinical Neuropsychologist, 8*(2), 219–238. doi:10.1080/138540 49408401559

British Psychological Society. (2007). *Guidelines for the employment of assistant psychologists.* Leicester: British Psychological Society.

British Psychological Society. (2010). *Additional guidance for clinical psychology training programmes: Guidelines on clinical supervision.* Leicester: British Psychological Society.

British Psychological Society. (2011a). *Guidelines for clinical psychology services.* Retrieved from https://www1.bps.org.uk/system/files/Public%20files/Dclinicalpsycho logist/cat-804.pdf

British Psychological Society. (2011b). *Good practice guidelines on the use of psychological formulation.* Leicester: British Psychological Society.

British Psychological Society. (2012a). *Guidance on activity for clinical psychologists: Relevant factors and the function and utility of job plans.* Leicester: British Psychological Society.

British Psychological Society (Division of Neuropsychology). (2012b). *Competency framework for the UK clinical neuropsychology profession.* Retrieved from https://www1.bps.org.uk/system/files/Public%20files/required_competences_for_clinical_neuropsychology.pdf

British Psychological Society. (2017). *Code of ethics and conduct.* Retrieved from www.bps.org.uk/sites/beta.bps.org.uk/files/News%20-%20Files/INF94%20Code%20Draft.pdf

Camp, C. J., Skrajner, M. J., Lee, M. M., & Judge, K. S. (2010). Cognitive assessment in late stage dementia. In P. A. Lichtenberg (Ed.), *Handbook of assessment in clinical gerontology* (2nd ed., pp. 531–555). London: Elsevier. doi:10.1016/B978-0-12-374961-1.10020-X

Collerton, D., & Domone, R. (2014). Cognitive assessment of people who may be developing dementia. In R. Guss (Ed.), *Clinical psychology in the early stage dementia care pathway* (pp. 31–38). Leicester: British Psychological Society.

FitzGerald, M. C. C., O'Keeffe, F., Carton, S., Coen, R. F., Kelly, S., & Dockree, P. (2017). Rehabilitation of emergent awareness of errors post traumatic brain injury: A pilot intervention. *Neuropsychological Rehabilitation,* 1–23. doi:10.1080/09602011.2017.13 36102

Folstein, M. F., Folstein, S. E., & McHugh, P. R. (1975). Mini-mental state: A practical method for grading the cognitive state of patients for the clinician. *Journal of Psychiatric Research, 12*(3), 189–198. doi:10.1037/t07757-000

Health and Care Professions Council. (2015). *Standards of proficiency – Practitioner psychologists.* Retrieved from www.hcpc-uk.org/assets/documents/10002963SOP_Practitioner_psychologists.pdf

Pegg, P. O., Auerbach, S. M., Seel, R. T., Buenaver, L. F., Kiesler, D. J., & Plybon, L. E. (2005). The impact of patient-centered information on patients' treatment satisfaction and outcomes in traumatic brain injury rehabilitation. *Rehabilitation Psychology, 50*(4), 366–374. doi:10.1037/0090-5550.50.4.366

Robertson, K., & Schmitter-Edgecombe, M. (2015). Self-awareness and traumatic brain injury outcome. *Brain Injury, 29*(7–8), 848–858. doi:10.3109/02699052.2015.1005135

Russo, A. C., Bush, S. S., & Rasin-Waters, D. (2013). Professional competence as the foundation for ethical neuropsychological practice with older adults. In L. D. Ravdin & H. L. Katzen (Eds.), *Handbook on the neuropsychology of aging and dementia* (pp. 217–223). New York, NY: Springer. doi:10.1007/978-1-4614-3106-0

Wilson, B., Cockburn, J., & Baddeley, A. D. (1985). *Rivermead behavioural memory test.* Flempton: Thames Valley Test Company.

Chapter 8

Clinical psychologists and the welfare benefits system

Rebecca Hutton

Summary points

- Experiences, both personal and professional, which are entangled with our political views, impact on the development of our professional identity throughout and beyond clinical psychology training.
- It is a vital part of competent practice for trainee and qualified clinical psychologists to engage with the wider systems within which they operate, including the welfare system and the political issues surrounding this.
- As well as engaging with such systems at an academic, systemic and political level, clinical psychologists can, at an individual level, involve themselves in directly supporting clients to navigate such systems; for example completing tasks such as filling out benefits forms with them.

The benefits system in context

The welfare system in the United Kingdom (UK) is currently undergoing one of its biggest ever changes; the introduction of Universal Credit (Department of Work and Pensions [DWP], 2018). Universal Credit replaces income support, jobseeker's allowance, Employment Support Allowance (ESA), housing benefit, working tax credit and child tax credit. At the time of writing, this programme is being rolled out in a phased manner across the country. This follows extensive changes in recent years to the financial support available for people with disabilities or long-term health needs, including the introduction of Personal Independence Payments (PIP) as a replacement for the Disability Living Allowance (DLA).

These changes follow a series of austerity programmes from the UK government. Beginning in 2008, following a period of economic recession, this included reductions in social spending and increased taxation. Austerity measures have been found to reduce the resources available to health services, while also having the most impact on vulnerable people such as those with insecure housing or employment, or those with physical or mental health problems, through increased unemployment, homelessness, poverty, food insecurity and rates of suicide or early mortality (Stuckler, Reeves, Loopstra, Karanikolos, & McKee, 2017).

A United Nations inquiry examining the cumulative impact of legislation, policies and measures adopted by the UK government in relation to social security schemes and how this affected the lives of people with disabilities highlighted that almost half a million people were moved off PIP and placed into the ESA group in 2015, after they were deemed 'fit to work' (United Nations, 2016). The United Nations concluded that these policies failed to uphold the rights of people with disabilities. Professor Phillip Alston (2018), a United Nations envoy, highlighted the impact of austerity policies on people living below the poverty line. He commented that "many aspects of the design and rollout of the programme have suggested that the DWP is more concerned with making economic savings and sending messages about lifestyles than responding to the multiple needs of those living with a disability, job loss, housing insecurity, illness, and the demands of parenting" (p. 5).

The drive to reduce state spending on welfare benefits payments has met with significant criticism, particularly in relation to the application and assessment process. Over 18% of all PIP claim decisions from 2013 to 2017 were overturned at appeal as they were found to have been incorrect (Parliament.uk, 2018). This figure does not capture those who did not appeal the decision. The criteria for PIP are also more stringent than DLA; a freedom of information request from Disability Rights UK (2017) found that 25% of people in receipt of a higher rate DLA mobility payment had their benefit reduced to the standard PIP mobility rate, while a further 23% lost their mobility rate entitlement altogether. This can mean a reduction of up to £3,000 in annual income, as well as the removal of the right to join the Motability scheme – leaving many people with disabilities who rented cars via the scheme less independent, unable to work or housebound. According to a survey by the Disability Benefits Consortium (2017), more than a third of people who had their benefits cut struggle to pay for food, rent and bills.

These changes have a disproportionately high impact on some of the more vulnerable people in society. Many people with disabilities face extra costs as a result of their impairment or condition; when taking into account costs such as adaptive equipment, specialist clothing, higher energy bills and higher insurance premiums, Touchet and Patel (2018) highlighted that people with disabilities face (on average) extra costs relating to their impairment or health condition of £570 per month.

The Disability Benefits Consortium (2017) also highlighted how the assessment process for disability benefits has been described as being too complicated, punitive and unfit for purpose, with 58% of respondents reporting that they did not feel that assessors understood their health condition and 79% of people stating that the assessment process for PIP had made their health worse by increasing stress and anxiety. Many 'invisible' conditions such as mental health problems or cognitive impairments are often overlooked, and the fluctuating nature of some conditions is often not taken into account: 22% of people claiming DLA due to mental health problems had their benefits reduced when they were assessed during the introduction of PIP, and a further 25% of people lost their benefits altogether (Full Fact,

2017). A report by Rethink (2017) highlighted how traumatising and anxiety-provoking the written and face-to-face components of the assessment process can be for people with mental health problems. The report also highlighted a clear need for further training around mental health for decision-makers.

More broadly, austerity policies and changes to the benefit system have been implicated in a dramatic increase in use of food banks in the UK. For example, Trussell Trust foodbanks reported yearly increases in provision of three-day emergency food supplies to families; they highlight that a growing proportion of referrals to food banks are due to benefits levels not covering the costs of essentials, with changes to or problems accessing benefits (including delayed payments or sanctions) seen as a fundamental driver in heightened food bank usage (Trussell Trust, 2018).

This is a broad overview of the distressing and demeaning situations that people accessing health and social care services are increasingly finding themselves in. Thinking about these issues became an important theme throughout my clinical psychology training, as I developed my professional identity as a clinical psychologist.

Clinical psychology and the benefits system

The increasing involvement in debate around austerity measures and the benefits system by clinical psychologists (McGrath, Griffin, & Mundy, 2015), has led me to continually reflect on our role in this system. Before I trained as a clinical psychologist, I worked as a mental health social worker. In this role, the financial wellbeing of a client was a priority and I was practically engaged in the tasks involved in supporting this: filling in forms, attending jobcentres, accessing emergency funding for those left without finance. On starting clinical psychology training, I began to reflect on the role of the clinical psychologist in supporting financial wellbeing or, more broadly, supporting clients to meet their basic needs. Perhaps some of the tasks detailed here would be considered inappropriate for a clinical psychologist, but maybe not all of them. Would you get practically involved in issues of poverty, finances and welfare? Would you support a client by filling in a benefits form?

There are a number of factors to consider when deciding whether to involve ourselves directly in any issues relating to benefits on a client level. During clinical psychology training, I was asked to fill out a DLA form (since replaced by PIP and due to be replaced again by Universal Credit) for a client I was working with. The request came from the client as there had been a lengthy wait for other professionals to support him/her with the form, while I had a designated time slot with him/her each week for therapy. However, this created something of an ethical dilemma; this appeared quite far removed from the work we had agreed to focus on and my understanding of my role in that relationship. The focus of this chapter is the manifestation of these issues within the context of people accessing adult mental health services in the NHS, however many of these considerations are relevant to any setting in which a clinical psychologist might work, such as with children and families, people with physical health problems, people with learning disabilities and people in the probation service.

Understanding mental health problems in context

At times, medical or diagnostic models of distress dominate our understandings. An alternative view, which I was introduced to during my social work training, is the social model of disability (e.g., Oliver & Sapey, 2006). In short, this presents the idea that an impairment (for example, a physical limitation or experiencing unusual beliefs) does not disable someone; society's reaction to that person and his/her impairment is what causes disability as we understand it. Instead of focusing on the functional impairments of the individual, the social model considers disability to be caused by the economic, cultural and environmental barriers which are faced by people with physical or cognitive impairments. For example, if a wheelchair user is not able to access a building, a social model perspective would argue that the person is only 'disabled' by the lack of reasonable accessibility adjustments or physical barriers preventing his/her access.

Alleviating distress involves looking at the individual and his/her social world. Access to a regular income is a good example of this; if a person does not have a reliable and adequate mechanism of financial support, this is likely to increase his/her distress. By supporting someone to find solutions, we can appreciate the person in his/her context and consider how to best meet his/her needs. If someone with a mental health problem has been denied benefits payments, he/she may become increasingly distressed, lose his/her independence and be unable to engage in positive activities which might improve mental wellbeing such as seeing friends or exercising. If we see the person as being the 'problem', then we are less likely to think about challenging the obstructions to social inclusion and wellbeing. By thinking about what 'disables' people, we can think about what we can do to break down those barriers.

Meeting basic needs as a clinical psychology concern

The Health and Care Professions Council (HCPC) guidance states that psychologists should understand their duty of care towards their clients (HCPC, 2010). A core purpose of clinical psychology is to support individuals to "maximise psychological and physical wellbeing" (Division of Clinical Psychology [DCP], 2011a, p. 3). Maslow's (1943) hierarchy of needs posits that only when an individual's basic physiological needs (e.g., shelter, warmth, food) are met can he/she strive for higher level needs like psychological wellbeing. If parents are unable to afford food or clothes for their children, would it be surprising if their stress levels and mood were affected? It is difficult to see how clients without sufficient income to eat regularly and heat their homes could even start to address any higher-level needs in psychological therapy.

Considering material issues is echoed in government mental health policy, which stresses the importance of tackling the underlying causes of mental health problems, such as poverty (HM Government, 2011). Supporting a client to claim benefits may be crucial in supporting him/her to meet his/her basic needs.

At the ground level: power, boundaries and the therapeutic alliance

When my client asked me for help filling in the DLA application form, I sought the opinion of my supervisor, who had a lot of experience of working in those settings. We reflected on the potential positive and negative consequences of supporting with the form.

Supervision in this case particularly focused on the therapeutic relationship, the boundaries of my role and the remit of clinical psychology as a profession. The therapeutic alliance between practitioner and service user is the most robust indicator of positive therapeutic outcomes, across treatment modalities and clinical presentations (Castonguay & Beutler, 2006). This influenced my decision-making because I was worried that not filling in the form would perhaps pose a challenge to a new therapeutic relationship, harming the chances of offering a helpful intervention.

However, clear boundaries are important in an effective relationship, which made me reflect on whether helping with financial issues was beyond the role of a clinical psychologist. Many would argue that it could be – other professionals (e.g., GPs, social workers) may be more typically expected to undertake this sort of role. This could be seen as outside the remit of psychological therapy, and, given the limitations on time and resources available within many psychology services, this could have a significant impact on the work.

However, supporting evidence or letters and the involvement in the application process from specialist professionals can often be deciding factors in an individual's application. Assessors rarely have extensive experience in mental health or psychological problems, and receive limited training on how to manage the complexity of such factors within the wider framework of a benefits application. On a practical level, many of the people we work with may struggle to engage with the application process – for example, people may lack access to the internet or have poor literacy skills, which will hamper their ability to complete an online claim form. People who have complex and longstanding problems with their mental health may understandably struggle with the stress and anxiety generated by the benefits application process; the involvement of a clinical psychologist in the process of applying for financial support may be crucial to their ability to complete an application.

Our role in this process might be to help highlight the extent of a person's difficulties, particularly if the individual struggles to communicate this accurately.

Camilleri and Hewitt (2016) highlight some examples of why people might have difficulty with doing this:

- Poor awareness of the severity of their difficulties due to cognitive problems or impaired insight.
- Anxiety throughout the assessment process making it more difficult for the person to assert or express themselves.
- Distress and shame triggered by discussing disability or mental health problems.
- Time pressures or lack of training/experience making it difficult to understand complex problems in the required level of detail.
- Problems with attending appointments and paying for supporting evidence where this is not covered by the organisation.
- Problems with accessing and engaging with services.

In addition to providing evidence of the extent of an individual's problems and highlighting triggers and vulnerability factors, clinical psychologists can be well placed to comment on how such factors might impact on a person's functioning and ability to engage with the assessment process, as well as highlighting any considerations or adaptations that could be made to improve the validity of the assessment and the robustness of the decision.

An important part of supervision for clinical psychologists is monitoring their own responses to situations that occur in practice (DCP, 2014). Throughout my practice I have found the helper's dance (Potter, 2013) a useful reference, particularly with issues where it is pertinent to consider whether something is within the role of a clinical psychologist and where interpersonal dynamics in the therapeutic relationship might influence my behaviour and decision making. It can be important to consider, for example, whether we are falling into the trap of being a *rescuer*; feeling like we need to meet all needs and fulfil all tasks, including for example form filling. I was aware that my previous care coordinator role, which was also in adult mental health, where I often felt responsible for all aspects of a client's care, was perhaps still influential in my practice. Clinical psychologists often offer therapy but would not engage with tasks beyond that, such as supporting clients to access benefits. Although I believe that my previous social work identity gives me a flexibility and pragmatism in clinical psychology practice, I am also aware of the potential trap of over involvement, when considering whether requested tasks are relevant in my role and where the limits and boundaries of a therapeutic relationship are.

The task of filling in the form together came at the beginning of therapy and opened up dialogue about needs and concerns; proving to be a useful therapeutic tool and an example of Rogers, Pilgrim and Lacey's (1993) finding that service users valued the human aspects of their contacts with professionals – feeling listened to and being treated with kindness and respect. Although filling in a DLA form may not be a task typically asked of a clinical psychologist, I felt it was crucial to the effectiveness of our ongoing work to improve this client's psychological wellbeing.

The act of form filling also fostered respect and acceptance. Increasingly in the UK, individuals who cannot work because of illness or disability are being constructed as undeserving and are vilified by the media and the public (Coote & Lyall, 2013). This is pertinent for those working in psychological professions, given that some investment in improving access to psychological therapies has been driven by initiatives aiming to get people with mental health problems back to work (Layard, Clark, Knapp, & Mayraz, 2007). Unfortunately, I have seen that this has led many clients to feel ashamed about applying for much needed financial support. Supporting the aforementioned client, and those I have worked with since, with issues around their financial situation has been part of conveying a message that they should not feel ashamed of needing some financial help during times of distress. It is important to support clients in a collaborative way through such a disempowering process. For example, asking them to write the application, but being there to offer suggestions about what they might be able to include and helping them to remember that the form's emphasis on symptoms and problems does not need to define every aspect of their life. Denying such help could easily perpetuate the shame around such issues.

At an individual level, it can be helpful to consider engaging with this kind of support, taking into account individual need and context. For example, considering whether very clear and firm boundaries are needed for therapeutic benefit, or whether those can be more flexible. It may be useful to ask if there are other professionals involved who could also help and contribute.

The professional identity of a clinical psychologist

Our professional identity, personal values and political views influence our decision making, particularly when decisions are complex or potentially controversial. Developing a professional identity as a clinical psychologist involves being influenced by new knowledge learned, new workplace experiences and interactions with others, particularly those who are teaching us, such as our supervisors. This developing professional identity will also be shaped by previous experience, which for me was my identity as a social worker. Therefore the emergence of my identity as a clinical psychologist involved change, replacement and merging of facets of both roles and identities, including a consideration of which concerns might be vital to the role of any caring professional.

A complicating issue in this is competence. Some may argue that welfare rights is not an area of expertise for clinical psychologists, and that there is a need to maintain focus on delivering psychological therapies without getting distracted by other concerns that should be dealt with by other professionals. Keeping professional knowledge and skills up to date and acting within the limits of those, and if necessary referring to a better placed practitioner, is a requirement of the HCPC (2012). BPS guidance suggests that clinical psychologists should be aware of their level of competence, knowledge and skill and work within it at all times (BPS, 2009). Awareness of working within a clinical psychologist's current range of skills should be a consideration of supervision (DCP, 2014). After discussing it in supervision, I decided that it was within my level of competence to help fill in the DLA form. In addition, I considered the professional identity I was trying to cultivate, merging the pragmatic approach of social work with the tasks of a clinical psychologist.

To ensure competence in such a task and to take account of any changes to the DLA form since practising social work, I decided to use a guide (Messere, 2013) to ensure that my knowledge was up to date; there is a lot of guidance available online around how to fill in such forms, and some examples are in the suggested reading list at the end of the chapter. I would argue that all clinical psychologists, with their level of education and training, have the skill to draw on such guidance to support their clients in filling in these forms.

Engaging in a positive and proactive way can also be helpful for the professional. A qualitative research project into the impact of austerity on the work of psychological therapists (Higson, Hodge, & Weatherhead, 2016) highlighted themes around threat, increased pressure, less focus on service users, being limited in what can be achieved and added emotional strain. By supporting a client to complete a benefits application or by writing a letter of support, clinical psychologists can hold a useful, hopeful and optimistic position in the work they do – these are key aspects of a positive professional identity.

Engaging at a wider level

There is also great potential for the impact of clinical psychologists becoming involved with these issues, both at an individual level, with tasks associated with navigating the benefits system and with wider, more contextual debates about the profession's identity and welfare reform.

The community psychology movement urges psychologists to take action to affect *first order* change (supporting individual, personal change) as well as *second order* change (trying to affect the systems involved with maintaining that problem) (Watzlawick, Weakland, & Fisch, 1974). Perhaps clinical psychology has evolved in a traditional sense to only address the former; Friedli suggests, "a rather limited, non-materialist or 'context lite' version of psychology" is dominant (2014, p. 11). On an individual level, this might involve considering with clients any difficulties in their lives, such as financial issues, that are affecting their mental wellbeing. Clinical psychologists should consider with the client whether those issues need to be addressed either before, or alongside, therapeutic intervention. However, clinical psychologists should also mobilise to try to bring about second order change, for example by getting involved in policy, politics and public health movements (Cooke, 2014).

There are increasing examples of such engagement. A clinical psychology–led group recently contributed to the DWP enquiry into fitness to work assessments (Weatherhead, 2014). Groups like *Psychologists for Social Change* also work towards increasing awareness of the psychological impact of social issues, such as austerity and the resulting poverty and distress (McGrath et al., 2015). The DCP leadership framework instructs that trainees should develop their political awareness within their organisation (DCP, 2011b). This underscores the importance of clinical psychologists being politically engaged as a part of their role as clinical leaders within the NHS to help support a move away from focusing only on delivering individual psychological interventions which are detached from these broader societal considerations.

Conclusion

Through my experiences of working in mental health services, I have become more aware of the systemic importance of debates about welfare reforms at a societal level and the need for clinical psychology to weigh in on such debates. While campaigning for all-encompassing change is necessary (and inspiring), I have realised that, at an individual level, clinical psychologists should be able to support clients with things that can contribute to their distress – such as navigating an increasingly complex and evolving welfare benefits system.

This may involve rethinking the traditional role boundaries and professional identity of a clinical psychologist, in order to directly address the societal influences on mental wellbeing. Professional identity, which is influenced by a clinical psychologist's experiences prior to and during training, is the vehicle that enables them to get involved in such issues. For this to happen, the profession must recognise the importance of engaging with these issues at individual and systemic levels. As a trainee clinical psychologist, I learned that I was able to challenge existing ways of working and support my clients in ways which were consistent with my developing professional identity. This is something I have taken into my qualified career.

Within the context of austerity politics and the impending changes to the welfare benefits system, clinical psychology can be a profession that stands away from practical, messy issues such as welfare benefits, even when we know that this has a significant impact on the physical and mental wellbeing of the people we work with. Perhaps instead, we can be willing to work flexibly and occasionally get our hands dirty.

Suggested further reading

Friedli, L. (2014). Reflections on the role of psychology in public health and workfare. *Clinical Psychology Forum, 256*, 11–15.

McGrath, L., Griffin, V., & Mundy, E. (2015). *The psychological impact of austerity: A briefing paper*. London: Psychologists Against Austerity. Retrieved from https://psychagainstausterity.files.wordpress.com/2015/03/paa-briefing-paper.pdf

Potter, S. (2013). 'The Helpers' dance'. In J. Lloyd & P. Clayton (Eds.), *Cognitive analytic therapy for people with learning disabilities and their carers* (pp. 89–95). London: Jessica Kingsley.

Tew, J. (2011). *Social models of mental distress*. London: Palgrave Macmillan.

Watts, J. (2017). *Supporting claimants: A practical guide*. Retrieved from http://asylummagazine.org/2018/08/supporting-claimants-a-practical-guide-by-jay-watts/

Westcountry Community Psychology. (2017). *Guidance on writing a good letter of support for PIP or ESA applications by clients with mental health difficulties or disabilities.* Retrieved from https://citizensadviceteignbridge.org.uk/wp-content/uploads/Med_Evidence_WCP_Guidance_final_14dec.pdf

References

Alston, P. (2018). *Statement on visit to the United Kingdom, by Professor Philip Alston, United Nations.* United Nations Human Rights, Office of the High Commissioner. Retrieved from www.ohchr.org/Documents/Issues/Poverty/EOM_GB_16Nov2018.pdf

British Psychological Society. (2009). *Code of ethics and conduct.* Leicester: British Psychological Society.

Camilleri, K., & Hewitt, L. (2016). *Getting off the fence about the benefits system.* Retrieved from https://www1.bps.org.uk/system/files/user-files/Division%20of%20Clinical%20Psychology/public/Getting%20off%20the%20fence%20about%20benefits%20presentation_DCP%20SW.pdf

Castonguay, L. G., & Beutler, L. E. (2006). Common and unique principles of therapeutic change: What do we know and what do we need to know? In L. G. Castonguay & L. E. Beutler (Eds.), *Principles of therapeutic change that work* (pp. 353–369). New York, NY: Oxford University Press.

Cooke, A. (2014). A response: So what do we need to do? *Clinical Psychology Forum, 256,* 22–25.

Coote, A., & Lyall, S. (2013, 11 April). Strivers v skivers: Real life's not like that at all. *The Guardian.* Retrieved from www.theguardian.com/commentisfree/2013/apr/11/strivers-v-skivers-divisive-notion

Department for Work and Pensions. (2018). *Universal credit.* Retrieved from www.gov.uk/universal-credit

Disability Benefits Consortium. (2017). *Supporting those who need it most? Evaluating personal independence payment.* Retrieved from https://disabilitybenefitsconsortium.files.wordpress.com/2017/09/supporting-those-who-need-it-most-full-report.pdf

Disability Rights UK. (2017). *Half of DLA claimants lose their higher mobility rate support on moving to PIP.* Retrieved from www.disabilityrightsuk.org/news/2017/july/half-dla-claimants-lose-their-higher-mobility-rate-support-moving-pip

Division of Clinical Psychology. (2011a). *The core purpose and philosophy of the profession.* Leicester: The British Psychological Society.

Division of Clinical Psychology. (2011b). *Clinical psychology leadership development framework.* Leicester: British Psychological Society.

Division of Clinical Psychology. (2014). *Division of clinical psychology policy on supervision.* Leicester: British Psychological Society.

Friedli, L. (2014). Reflections on the role of psychology in public health and workfare. *Clinical Psychology Forum, 256,* 11–15.

Full Fact. (2017). *Are people with mental health conditions now receiving higher disability benefit payments?* Retrieved from https://fullfact.org/economy/are-people-mental-health-conditions-now-receiving-higher-disability-benefit-payments/

Health and Care Professions Council. (2010). *Standards of proficiency: Practitioner psychologists.* London: HCPC.

Health and Care Professions Council. (2012). *Standards of conduct, performance and ethics.* London: HCPC.

Higson, H., Hodge, S., & Weatherhead, S. (2016). *Explorations of mental health professionals' views on hope and austerity: The synergy of a paradox?* (PhD thesis). Lancaster University, London. Retrieved from http://eprints.lancs.ac.uk/84856/

HM Government. (2011). *No health without mental health*. Retrieved from www.gov.uk/government/publications/the-mental-health-strategy-for-england

Layard, R., Clark, D., Knapp, M., & Mayraz, G. (2007). Cost – Benefit analysis of psychological therapy. *National Institute Economic Review, 202*, 90–98. doi:10.1177/0027950107086171

Maslow, A. H. (1943). A theory of human motivation. *Psychological Review, 50*(4), 370–396. doi:10.1037/h0054346

McGrath, L., Griffin, V., & Mundy, E. (2015). *The psychological impact of austerity: A briefing paper*. London: Psychologists Against Austerity. Retrieved from https://psychagainstausterity.files.wordpress.com/2015/03/paa-briefing-paper.pdf

Messere, T. (2013). *The big book of benefits and mental health* (13th ed.). London: Mind Publications.

Oliver, O., & Sapey, B. (2006). *Social work with disabled people*. Basingstoke: Palgrave Macmillan.

Parliament.UK. (2018). *PIP and ESA assessments: Disputed decisions*. Retrieved from https://publications.parliament.uk/pa/cm201719/cmselect/cmworpen/829/82908.htm#footnote-092

Potter, S. (2013). The Helpers' dance. In J. Lloyd & P. Clayton (Eds.), *Cognitive analytic therapy for people with learning disabilities and their carers* (pp. 89–95). London: Jessica Kingsley.

Rethink. (2017). *It's broken her – Our report into WCA and PIP benefits*. Retrieved from www.rethink.org/get-involved/policy/its-broken-her-wca-and-pip-report

Rogers, A., Pilgrim, D., & Lacey, R. (1993). *Experiencing psychiatry: Users' views of services*. Basingstoke: Palgrave Macmillan.

Stuckler, D., Reeves, A., Loopstra, R., Karanikolos, M., & McKee, M. (2017). Austerity and health: The impact in the UK and Europe. *European Journal of Public Health, 27*(4), 18–21. doi:10.1093/eurpub/ckx167

Touchet, A., & Patel, M. (2018). *The disability price tag*. London: Scope. Retrieved from www.scope.org.uk/Scope/media/Documents/Publication%20Directory/The-disability-price-tag-Policy-report.pdf?ext=.pdf

Trussell Trust. (2018). *End of year stats*. Retrieved from www.trusselltrust.org/news-and-blog/latest-stats/end-year-stats/

United Nations. (2016). *Inquiry concerning the United Kingdom of Great Britain and Northern Ireland carried out by the committee under article 6 of the optional protocol to the convention*. Retrieved from www.ohchr.org/Documents/HRBodies/CRPD/CRPD.C.15.R.2.Rev.1-ENG.doc

Watzlawick, P., Weakland, J., & Fisch, R. (1974). *Change: Principles of problem formation and problem resolution*. New York, NY: Norton.

Weatherhead, S. (2014). The media-based stigmatization of people who access benefits. *Clinical Psychology Forum, 257*, 8–10.

Chapter 9

Supervision

The professional and ethical issues facing trainee clinical psychologists

Nicola Edwards, Helena Coleman and Javier Malda-Castillo

Summary points

- Supervision is a complex and multifaceted relationship, which can be challenging to manage throughout clinical psychology training and beyond.
- In supervision, trainees may feel anxious about presenting themselves as competent and skilled, while also highlighting areas of development and being open to feedback. It can often feel like there is a lack of space to fail, highlight weaknesses or ask for support.
- Honesty and open communication is key in facilitating the development of supportive, effective and safe supervision.

Supervision within clinical psychology aims to monitor the quality of a practitioner's performance to ensure safety and quality care for service users, while providing a supportive space for the development of skills and expertise (British Psychological Society [BPS], 2008; Division of Clinical Psychology [DCP], 2014). Proctor's (1987) framework for supervision identifies three broad components to supervision:

- *Formative* – learning and skill development.
- *Normative* – supporting managerial accountability and professional standards.
- *Restorative* – supporting the supervisee to mitigate the emotional impact of their work.

Supervision can be varied and might include individual, group or peer supervision. During clinical psychology training, one-to-one supervision with a qualified clinical psychologist is the most common experience. For trainee clinical psychologists, a qualified clinical psychologist will oversee their work and supervise them on their clinical placements, usually through weekly meetings of 60–90 minutes where clinical work is discussed. Additionally, some supervisors provide informal supervision and can be approached outside of the agreed supervision slot. All practicing clinical psychologists must utilise supervision throughout their career (BPS, 2006).

Many healthcare professionals will have been involved in a form of supervision. It is not possible to provide an in-depth discussion of all ethical and professional issues that may arise within supervision in this chapter, however in this chapter we will introduce some ideas to consider from the perspective of being a trainee clinical psychologist. The experience of supervision as a trainee clinical psychologist may be different to other professional groups; there is an expectation that this will involve aspects of operational/line management supervision, professional supervision and clinical supervision (see DCP, 2014, and Creaner, 2014, for further definition and discussion).

In the supervisory space, ethical and professional challenges, clinical discussions and/or organisational issues can be discussed. These issues could include breaches of confidentiality, risk management or consideration of professional boundaries. How a clinician copes with these situations, and how supervision is utilised within that process, has been found to shape future practice (Barnett, 2007), illustrating the impact effective supervision can have on the development of a professional identity. Gottlieb, Robinson and Younggren (2007) state that trainees are still developing their concept of ethics, and therefore need extra support and guidance on how to manage and navigate professional challenges through regular supervision.

The multifaceted nature of supervision

Working in mental health settings can include working with people who have experienced trauma. This can result in unsettling feelings for the clinician which may be challenging to manage (Wilson, 2013). As a trainee, these feelings can be overwhelming, and one might need a space to discuss and make sense of the experience; supervision could be this safe space. Supervisees may also need to explore aspects of their personal life during supervision, as certain issues may evoke a strong emotional reaction for a supervisee that warrants further discussion (Olk & Friedlander, 1992). At this point, the supervisee is adopting a role similar to that of a client and thus needs to find the balance between being reflective and open, without inappropriately using supervision as personal therapy (BPS, 2008).

The supervisory relationship is multifaceted and complex. Supervision for trainee clinical psychologists is not limited to the provision of emotional support and includes a range of tasks that need to be completed such as discussing risk management guidelines, information governance procedures, outcome measures and discharges, assessment or referral letters. With 60–90 minutes of weekly supervision and with a caseload of six to eight clients, one can start to wonder how much time is left in supervision to make sense of the emotional impact of working with vulnerable people. We have found it beneficial to discuss a clear agenda at the outset, and let supervisors know that we would like specified time (e.g., 15–20 minutes/weekly) to discuss difficult personal reactions to clinical work.

Conflict within the supervisory relationship

As with any relationship, conflict can occur within supervisory relationships. This can make it incredibly difficult to discuss emotional responses to clinical work; this can leave trainees in a vulnerable and exposed place. Supervisees have been described throughout the literature as the vulnerable party in an unequal power relationship, which increases the potential risk of exploitation (Gottlieb et al., 2007). Biaggio, Paget and Chenoweth (1997) stated that tutors and supervisors are ultimately responsible for maintaining professional and ethical working relationships. However, stating that one member of the relationship has more responsibility appears to reinforce this power imbalance. Some conflict within supervision can be necessary, and, at times, beneficial in aiding the development of the supervisee (Nelson, Barnes, Evans, & Triggiano, 2008). Supervisees who had experienced conflict were reported to have learned valuable lessons from these experiences, for example finding coping strategies they were not aware they had (Nelson & Friedlander, 2001).

However, these experiences can also negatively impact wellbeing and reduce a trainee's ability to place their trust in others (Nelson & Friedlander, 2001). The emotional stress caused by difficult supervisory relationships is concerning, and the long-term effect that these experiences have on future practice is unclear. Some courses emphasise the importance of a mentorship for trainees who have experienced conflicts with their placement supervisors as a means of supporting the trainee with their emotional wellbeing. A positive relationship with a mentor can be just as important to a trainee as a supervisory relationship on placement and could give the trainee the opportunity to digest difficult feelings and use them to aid development within a safe, less structured, learning environment.

Discussing conflict and difficulties within the relationship could be felt as being 'high risk' for trainee clinical psychologists. Clinical supervisors are ultimately responsible for whether a trainee passes or fails a placement. Although the training course has the final decision, it is likely they will take the recommendation of the supervisor as a means of assessing the trainee's competencies. It may be perceived as unwise to raise certain issues within supervision as this could affect the outcome of a trainee's placement assessment. However, some may feel that it is important to take this risk. We would encourage trainees to recognise that their voice is important and, from this, have the courage to raise issues with their supervisors and programme team as openly and honestly as they can.

The emotional impact of supervision

The power imbalances within a supervisory relationship can resemble that of a parent-child; one role holds more power (i.e., parent/supervisor) and is responsible for the more vulnerable and less powerful party (i.e., child/supervisee). Supervision can elicit emotional reactions in both trainees and supervisors, which may be linked with their previous experiences of professional and personal relationships (Dickson, Moberly, Marshall, & Reilly, 2011). This can be challenging; supervisees can become overly anxious about doing well or not disappointing their supervisor, or they could experience supervisors as critical or authoritarian. Supervision can also be an anxiety-provoking experience for the supervisor; he/she holds clinical responsibility for any work completed by the trainee and his/her professional registration is at risk if anything goes wrong.

Attachment theory proposes that, through our experiences of relating to other people, we all develop a threat system that is activated in stressful situations and can lead to a wide range of both helpful and unhelpful behaviours (Bowlby, 1969; Ainsworth, Blehar, Waters, & Wall, 1978). These attachment systems accompany us throughout life and may become evident when in a new and complex interpersonal relationship, such as individual supervision.

As an example, imagine a trainee clinical psychologist who had little personal experience of being taken seriously or listened to during his/her upbringing. This person might have learned to feel that his/her worries, thoughts or opinions were not important, therefore dismissing or paying little attention to them. In the supervisory relationship, he/she might present him/herself as pleasant and compliant, following the wishes and needs of the supervisor and avoiding communicating personal opinions. However, if the trainee disagreed with his/her supervisor's advice about discharging one of his/her clients, the trainee might not feel able to communicate this in supervision, and neglect to tell the supervisor about concerns he/she had about heightened levels of risk. The supervisor might assume that he/she both made an appropriate clinical decision, yet the risks to the client have not been managed properly. The trainee might feel guilty or worried about his/her client but feel unable to express this. Repeated experiences of this kind might have a significant emotional impact on the trainee, and his/her anxiety could make it difficult for him/her to share his/her opinions and feelings in subsequent supervisions, perpetuating the cycle.

Given the complexity of supervisory relationships within clinical psychology training, and the need for integration of both honest reflection and direct (often developmental) feedback, being supervised can be an exposing and anxiety-provoking process. We would encourage trainees engaging in supervision to think about their own interpersonal relationships, and to think about how this might play out within supervision. To minimise the development of problems in a supervisory relationship – or to reflect on ruptures that have developed within a supervisory relationship – we offer the following suggestions:

- Consider using supervisory style questionnaires such as the *Supervisory Styles Inventory* (Friedlander & Ward, 1984) as a tool to support reflection.
- Consider developing a supervisory contract that includes regular review slots in which the process of supervision can be discussed. This can increase the chances of having a more positive experience (BPS, 2008; Goodyear, Crego, & Johnston, 1992), and can include specific agreements (e.g., how best to give/receive feedback).

- Consider establishing a mentoring relationship with a qualified professional outside the course separate to the evaluative processes embedded within the programme.

Supervision and assessment

Supervision within clinical psychology training is a quality assurance for ensuring the competence and clinical skills of the trainee. Supervisors have an ethical and professional obligation to monitor and discuss the competence of supervisees (Johnson, 2008). During supervision, both parties have the combined responsibility of carefully balancing diverse and often conflicting roles (Johnson, 2007, Johnson, 2008; Kaslow, Falender, & Grus, 2012). This is particularly important for clinical psychology training because supervisors must provide guidance and support, while simultaneously evaluating the supervisee's work to protect the public from incompetent practice (Biaggio et al., 1997).

The situation discussed earlier presented a dilemma about the emotional impact of supervision in addition to the assessment and evaluative components of this relationship. The supervisee withheld information, which increased the risk to the client. However this also hindered the trainee's learning and development; it is difficult for a supervisor to support a trainee with problems and dilemmas that he/she is simply unaware of (Ladany, Hill, Corbett, & Nutt, 1996), yet a trainee might not always feel safe or comfortable raising things he/she has not done well or is uncertain about. The trainee's future career could be compromised if professional competences have not been developed; once training is completed, he/she is responsible for his/her own practice. And of course, the safety of clients should always take precedence and override any anxiety about raising concerns (HCPC, 2008; Vasquez, 1992).

In our experience, supervisors who normalise mistakes and encourage trainees to have a positive risk-taking stance contribute to creating an atmosphere of transparency and honesty, leading to richer learning (Nelson et al., 2008). It is also important to note that trainees should not be working beyond their level of competence, as this would be regarded as unethical practice (BPS, 2008, 2009). Throughout training it may be helpful to discuss with supervisors your previous experience and how prepared you feel to undertake specific clinical work before agreeing to do so. While this can be an exposing process, learning to sit with this vulnerability is a core skill required for clinical psychology training.

Another helpful approach is to agree with the supervisor that positive and developmental feedback will be given during each supervision session, as a routine part of the learning process. As we have progressed through training, we have progressively felt more comfortable with developmental feedback, rather than experiencing this as being criticised or attacked. This contracting approach can also help supervisors reduce their reluctance to address a trainee's competence, which can be underpinned by a fear of jeopardising the trainee's future career (Forrest, Elman, Gizara, & Vacha-Haase, 1999). By providing regular developmental feedback, supervisors reduce the chances of exposing clients to incompetent practice, placing members of the public at risk and jeopardising their own clinical integrity (Jacobs et al., 2011). For the trainee, this can reduce anxiety around the assessment components of the supervisory relationship and encourage transparency and openness.

The importance of observation

Although clinical supervisors are expected to observe or work jointly with trainees at the outset of a placement, trainee clinical psychologists work mostly independently. Being observed once or twice at the start of a new placement may be insufficient to allow an appropriate assessment of competence. It may also limit the amount of direct feedback a supervisor can give to a trainee as part of their learning and development.

As a result, there is now an increasing emphasis on recording therapy sessions to structure supervision, with some training programmes incorporating this into mandatory assessment (BPS, 2015). Although this is relatively novel for trainee clinical psychologists, practitioners in other disciplines (e.g., cognitive-behavioural therapy [CBT], family/systemic therapy and post-qualified modalities such as Video Interactive Guidance [VIG]) have been engaging in this kind of live supervision for many years. Using video recordings in supervision raises both challenges and opportunities to contribute to the supervisory experience, while adding another layer of complexity around how feedback is given and received.

When discussing the option of video recording with clients (to establish informed consent), we have noticed that this can cause some anxiety. While it may be understandable for the client to be reluctant about being filmed, we would encourage trainees to reflect also on their own emotional reactions to this process. Some trainees experience feelings of shame and humiliation when presenting therapy sessions in live supervision; anxiety about the supervisor criticising their skills or approach may lead to some resistance in being filmed. Consciously or unconsciously, they may raise the client's anxiety levels as a result through the way they introduce the concept of filming sessions or through the way they respond to questions about the process.

Despite the understandable anxiety that it can cause, we feel that sharing video recordings with supervisors can be a positive experience, helping with the development of required competencies (HCPC, 2015). It offers trainees the opportunity to show strengths and develop confidence through the process of getting feedback on their clinical work from a more experienced clinician. When managed compassionately, live supervision can help to highlight areas of development necessary for a safe and effective learning environment (HCPC, 2017).

We advise that prospective trainees dedicate some time to thinking about and discussing with their supervisor the following questions:

- How do I feel about videoing my sessions?
- What impact might this have on the clients I am working with?

- What am I most worried about?
- What support is available to me to manage this?
- How will I manage the feedback I get?
- How can I best explain to my client that this is a normal and helpful process, while also respecting their right to refuse?
- What could I gain from videoing my sessions?

Conclusion

In supervision, trainees need to present themselves as competent and skilled, while also highlighting areas of development and being open to feedback. It can often feel like there is a lack of space to fail, highlight weaknesses or ask for support. Trainees could feel the need to demonstrate expertise in areas where they have not yet developed, leading to significant concerns in terms of maintaining the safety and wellbeing of clients. For supervision to work effectively, it should be individualised, and supervisors should adapt their style, pace and supervisory model to suit the supervisee's needs and progress (Barnett, 2007). We would encourage trainees to actively engage with the development of these relationships to ensure they get the most out of them. Honesty is a recurrent theme throughout the literature (Pettifor, McCarron, Schoepp, Stark, & Stewart, 2011), highlighting the importance of open communication within supervision which is supportive, effective and safe.

Suggested further reading

Creaner, M. (2014). *Getting the best out of supervision in counselling and psychotherapy: A guide for the supervisee*. London: Sage.

Dickson, J. M., Moberly, N. J., Marshall, Y., & Reilly, J. (2011). Attachment style and its relationship to working alliance in the supervision of British clinical psychology trainees. *Clinical Psychology & Psychotherapy, 18*(4), 322–330. doi:10.1002/cpp.715

Fleming, I., & Steen, L. (Eds.). (2013). *Supervision and clinical psychology: Theory, practice and perspectives*. London: Routledge.

References

Ainsworth, M. S., Blehar, M. C., Waters, E., & Wall, S. (1978). *Patterns of attachment: A psychological study of the strange situation* (1st ed.). Hillsdale, NJ: Erlbaum.

Barnett, J. E. (2007). In search of the effective supervisor. *Professional Psychology: Research and Practice, 38*(3), 268–275. doi:10.1037/0735-7028.38.3.268

Biaggio, M., Paget, T. L., & Chenoweth, M. S. (1997). A model for ethical management of faculty-student dual relationships. *Professional Psychology: Research and Practice, 28*(2), 184–189. doi:10.1037/0735-7028.28.2.184

Bowlby, J. (1969). *Attachment and loss. Vol. 1: Attachment* (1st ed.). New York, NY: Basic Books.

British Psychological Society. (2006). *Division of clinical psychology: Continued supervision policy document.* Leicester: The British Psychological Society. Retrieved from www.queenmarysroehampton.nhs.uk/working/supervision/Supervision%20Documents/Psychological%20Society.pdf

British Psychological Society. (2008). *Professional practice board: Generic professional practice guidelines.* Leicester: British Psychological Society. Retrieved from www.bps.org.uk/sites/default/files/documents/generic_professional_practice_guidelines.pdf

British Psychological Society. (2009). *Code of ethics and conduct.* Leicester: British Psychological Society. Retrieved from www.bps.org.uk/sites/default/files/documents/code_of_ethics_and_conduct.pdf

British Psychological Society. (2015). *Standards for the accreditation of doctoral programmes in clinical psychology.* Retrieved from https://www1.bps.org.uk/system/files/Public%20files/PaCT/clinical_accreditation_2015_web.pdf

Division of Clinical Psychology. (2014). *DCP policy on supervision.* Retrieved from https://www1.bps.org.uk/system/files/Public%20files/inf224_dcp_supervision.pdf

Forrest, L., Elman, N., Gizara, S., & Vacha-Haase, T. (1999). Trainee impairment: A review of identification, remediation, dismissal, and legal issues. *Counseling Psychologist, 27*(5), 627–686. doi:10.1177/0011000099275001

Friedlander, M. L., & Ward, L. G. (1984). Development and validation of the supervisory styles inventory. *Journal of Counseling Psychology, 31*(4), 541–557. doi:10.1037/0022-0167.31.4.541

Goodyear, R. K., Crego, C. A., & Johnston, M. W. (1992). Ethical issues in the supervision of student research: A study of critical incidents. *Professional Psychology: Research and Practice, 23*(3), 203–210. doi:10.1037/0735-7028.23.3.203

Gottlieb, M. C., Robinson, K., & Younggren, J. N. (2007). Multiple relations in supervision: Guidance for administrators, supervisors, and students. *Professional Psychology: Research and Practice, 38*(3), 241–247. doi:10.1037/0735-7028.38.3.241

Health and Care Professions Council. (2008). *Standards of conduct, performance and ethics.* London: Health and Care Professions Council. Retrieved from www.hcpc-uk.org/publications/standards/index.asp?id=38

Health and Care Professions Council. (2015). *Standards of proficiency – Practitioner psychologists.* London: Health and Care Professions Council. Retrieved from www.hcpc-uk.org/assets/documents/10002963SOP_Practitioner_psychologists.pdf

Health and Care Professions Council. (2017). *Standards of education and training.* London: Health and Care Professions Council. Retrieved from www.hcpc-uk.org/assets/documents/10000BCF46345Educ-Train-SOPA5_v2.pdf

Jacobs, S. C., Huprich, S. K., Grus, C. L., Cage, E. A., Elman, N. S., Forrest, L., ... Kaslow, N. J. (2011). Trainees with professional competency problems: Preparing trainers for difficult but necessary conversations. *Training and Education in Professional Psychology, 5*(3), 175–184. doi:10.1037/a0024656

Johnson, W. B. (2007). Transformational supervision: When supervisors mentor. *Professional Psychology: Research and Practice, 38*(3), 259–267. doi:10.1037/0735-7028.38.3.259

Johnson, W. B. (2008). Can psychologists find a way to stop the hot potato game? *Professional Psychology: Research and Practice, 39*(6), 589–593. doi:10.1037/a0014264

Kaslow, N. J., Falender, C. A., & Grus, C. L. (2012). Valuing and practicing competency-based supervision: A transformational leadership perspective. *Training and Education in Professional Psychology, 6*(1), 47–54. doi:10.1037/a0026704

Ladany, N., Hill, C. E., Corbett, M. M., & Nutt, E. A. (1996). Nature, extent, and importance of what psychotherapy trainees do not disclose to their supervisors. *Journal of Counselling Psychology*, *43*(1), 10–24. doi:10.1037/0022-0167.43.1.10

Nelson, M. L., Barnes, K. L., Evans, A. L., & Triggiano, P. J. (2008). Working with conflict in clinical supervision: Wise supervisors' perspectives. *Journal of Counselling Psychology*, *55*(2), 172–184. doi:10.1037/0022-0167.55.2.172

Nelson, M. L., & Friedlander, M. L. (2001). A close look at conflictual supervisory relationships: The trainee's perspective. *Journal of Counselling Psychology*, *48*(4), 384–395. doi:10.1037/0022-0167.48.4.384

Olk, M. E., & Friedlander, M. L. (1992). Trainees' experiences of role conflict and role ambiguity in supervisory relationships. *Journal of Counselling Psychology*, *39*(3), 389–397. doi:10.1037/0022-0167.39.3.389

Pettifor, J., McCarron, M. C. E., Schoepp, G., Stark, C., & Stewart, D. (2011). Ethical supervision in teaching, research, practice, and administration. *Canadian Psychology*, *52*(3), 198–205. doi:10.1037/a0024549

Proctor, B. (1987). Supervision: A co-operative exercise in accountability. In M. Marken & M. Payne (Eds.), *Enabling and ensuring: Supervision in practice* (pp. 21–34). Leicester: National Youth Bureau and the Council for Education and Training in Youth and Community Work.

Vasquez, M. J. T. (1992). Psychologist as clinical supervisor: Promoting ethical practice. *Professional Psychology: Research and Practice*, *23*(3), 196–202. doi:10.1037/0735-7028.23.3.196

Wilson, P. T. (2013). *Reflective practice: Bridging the gap between theory and practice*. London: The King's Fund Library, Institute of Group Analysis. doi:10.1037/0735-7028.23.3.196

Chapter 10

Should clinical psychologists be political?

Masuma Rahim and Anne Cooke

Summary points

- People who develop mental health problems are likely to experience adversity, prejudice and social exclusion, both early in life, and as a consequence of their psychological difficulties.
- While individual therapeutic work has value, it does not tackle the causes of distress, which are often rooted in social, historical and economic systems.
- By taking a more overtly political stance clinical psychologists can be part of wider systemic change.

It is impossible to divorce psychology from politics.

Firstly, people's social circumstances have a profound effect on their mental health and wellbeing (Harper, 2016). Unsurprisingly, adversity – for example trauma, poverty, prejudice or social isolation – substantially increases the likelihood of developing enduring mental health problems (Felitti et al., 1998).

Secondly, the converse is also true. Those of us with mental health problems are more likely to live in poverty, to be socially isolated and to have poor physical health (Barry & Jenkins, 2007).

Thirdly, despite being more likely to need them, people from marginalised sectors of society often get a poor deal from NHS mental health services. This is partly because institutional racism and other forms of discrimination have been shown to affect the manner in which people from minority backgrounds are treated and the extent to which they are offered appropriate support (Fernando, 2017; Rogers & Pilgrim, 2014), and partly because people from these sectors are underrepresented amongst mental health workers, and perhaps particularly amongst clinical psychologists (Rogers & Pilgrim, 2014).

Fourthly, there is the issue of prejudice and discrimination in relation to mental health problems. Despite national anti-stigma campaigns such as *Time to Change*, negative attitudes persist towards those with mental health diagnoses (Evans-Lacko, Corker, Williams, Henderson, & Thornicroft, 2014). Shame and fear of prejudice are major reasons for people disengaging from mental health services, or for not seeking help in the first place. Some 75% of people who experience psychological distress fail to get the help they need (Mental Health Foundation, 2016). There is also evidence that prejudice and discrimination affect people's chances of getting a job, and that they influence the debate about how healthcare budgets should be allocated (Sharac, Mccrone, Clement, & Thornicroft, 2010). While it's easy to blame the media for reporting misinformation and perpetuating stereotypes, Anne Cooke makes the point that, as professionals with substantial knowledge at our disposal, we can hardly blame laypeople for reporting inaccurate information unless we proactively provide them with more robust and nuanced alternatives (Cooke, 1999).

But is this the role of psychologists? Historically, we have tended to work in NHS settings rather than in policy (Longwill, 2015). In times of tightening budgets and downgrading of posts it is understandable that some people simply want to carry on with the day-job and avoid rocking the boat. But in this chapter, we argue that psychologists are not only equipped, but arguably have an ethical duty, to work much more 'beyond therapy' (Beyond the Therapy Room, 2017).

Firstly, there is much about our UK mental health services that needs to change. Over the past 30 years we have witnessed a dramatic increase in the number of psychiatric drugs prescribed (D. Campbell, 2017; Ilyas & Moncrieff, 2012). Within mental health services, medication is often the only thing on offer. Despite the fact that national guidelines recommend psychological interventions, only a fraction of people who use mental health services receive them (Mental Health Taskforce, 2016). The financial crash of 2008 and the austerity policies which followed have resulted in a decade of significant cuts to funding across health, education and social care. In some parts of the UK, these cuts mean that people are waiting up to two years for psychological therapy – and even then only if they are among the minority deemed appropriate to receive it (Cooper, 2018).

In our experience of working in community mental health teams we have observed, for example, that the people referred for therapy are often middle-class, white and educated, even if the local population has a very different demographic profile. It is clear to us that in many areas ethnic minorities and the less affluent have far less access to the services that we as psychologists provide. Even amongst those who do surmount the hurdles and manage to see a psychologist, many continue to live with long-term difficulties related to financial instability, inadequate housing and social exclusion (Fitch, Hamilton, Bassett, & Davey, 2011; Murali & Oyebode, 2004), none of which therapy is likely to resolve.

Despite the expansion of psychological therapy in the NHS under the auspices of the Improving Access to Psychological Therapies (IAPT) programme, the majority of IAPT services provide time-limited input designed for people who experience mild to moderate distress. Our experience is that long-term, sustained therapeutic input which is designed to work with people in complex circumstances is simply unavailable to most people reliant on the NHS, and very few have the resources to access it privately. Add to that the well-known problems associated with the dominance of the medical model (Cooke, Smythe, & Anscombe, submitted), it seems that the way we currently organise and deliver therapy services just doesn't work for many. Perhaps, then, the way we think about and practise clinical psychology has to change.

Secondly, we know that many so-called mental health problems are normal responses to the myriad social problems that many people have to survive on a daily basis. In the UK, people who live in poverty are more likely not only to smoke and to be obese, but also to be diagnosed with depression and anxiety (Friedli, 2009). Other forms of adversity, particularly early in life, also have profound consequences. Childhood exposure to abuse, domestic violence and neglect are associated with higher rates of substance use, aggression and psychosis, as well as increased risk of suicidality (Rahim, 2014). Nor are these experiences uncommon – in one study of 5,900 people, over half reported having had one of these experiences and a quarter reported two or more (Felitti et al., 1998). We know that prevention is better than cure – so why are we focused on offering individual therapy to casualties of a broken society rather than getting involved in the public health agenda? Even if you disagree with the notion that governments are ethically obliged to improve the wellbeing of citizens, it is almost always cheaper to address the factors which contribute to poor mental health than to try to treat difficulties once they occur.

The data are clear: deprivation, inequality and adversity lead to poorer outcomes across the lifespan and also limit the ways in which people are able to contribute to society. The loss does not occur purely at an individual level – if psychological distress prevents some of us from attaining the things most of us aspire to, such as good health, positive relationships and financial security, this affects our society as a whole. Clinical psychologists know this. We know it not just because we have the data but because our training allows us to understand the psychological impact of different types of adversity. So why do the majority of us just carry on working individually with those few lucky enough to get through the hurdles and make it into our therapy rooms? Why are we so reluctant to speak out? We will return to this question – and our vision of how things could be different – shortly.

It is inarguable that inequality adversely affects wellbeing, and that negative public perceptions of 'mental illness' are a huge problem for those affected, despite frequently being based on misinformation (try Googling 'psychosis' or 'schizophrenia', for example). It follows, then, that systemic problems require systemic – rather than individual – solutions (Rahim, 2017). We believe that clinical psychologists are ideally placed to have a positive impact at the systemic level. But how can early-career psychologists be part of a wider solution?

There is no one 'right' approach. People have different experiences, skills and resources, and each person's capacity to be involved in this – often extracurricular and unpaid – work will vary depending on myriad factors in both their personal and professional lives. But for those who agree that it is important that psychologists be involved, and who are willing to be part of it, there are a number of ways to do so. It's important to be clear that although we are arguing for greater political engagement amongst psychologists, we are not talking about our personal politics, or the political parties that we support. We acknowledge that different people have different political allegiances, and we believe that these issues should be held in mind by all those who work in the psychology professions without our personal beliefs getting in the way.

Understanding systems

Most importantly, we must understand the systems and structures which have created the problems we see in our society. Poverty, exclusion and injustice do not exist in a vacuum; social context is always rooted in an historical legacy. History does not generally feature very much in clinical psychology training courses, but it is vital that those of us who wish to engage in social activism educate ourselves. And although some of us have had to overcome barriers on our journey to becoming clinical psychologists, we must never forget that there are many who have found those barriers to be insurmountable. Furthermore, while there are several key writers with whom we should all be familiar – David Smail comes to mind here – we must not limit ourselves to learning only from fellow professionals. It is vital that we learn, primarily, from the people with direct experience of distress and oppression. Sometimes we need to put our knowledge and our qualifications to one side, and often we need to hear and reflect on things that are difficult. If we are to engage in this work we have to acknowledge that we are part of a system which oppresses people and takes away their rights (Rahim, 2017). We cannot speak truth to power if we cannot hear the truth ourselves.

Using knowledge to influence

We need to then use our knowledge to improve society. This can take the form both of grassroots work, as practised by community psychology, and of more formal roles, including lobbying government and standing for civic office. There is a common belief that public sector employees are prohibited from speaking out on political issues. This is a myth – of course we must not discriminate against service users with different political beliefs, but we should acknowledge that our work is intrinsically political. Furthermore, as citizens, we have the inalienable right to be politically engaged. The organisation *Psychologists for Social Change* (www.psychchange.org), who have written a number of position statements and open letters in response to government briefings, are a good example of this.

It is only by highlighting the psychological impact of issues such as housing, debt and welfare reform to those in positions of power that we can hope to bring about change. We know, for example, that there is a social housing crisis in the UK. We also know that unstable and unsuitable housing affects people in myriad ways, and is often a major factor in the development and maintenance of mental health problems. The government is only likely to take action to reverse this crisis if there is sufficient pressure from Members of Parliament, who in turn will prioritise the issues their constituents raise. If clinical psychologists began more actively engaging with our elected representatives we might start to see more debate – and perhaps even action – regarding the many social ills into which our daily conversations with those at the sharp end give us particular insight.

Making a stand

Crucially, we need to have principles that we are prepared to stand by. For us, one incontrovertible principle is that we actively make a stand against abuses of human rights. In the current UK context, this means being vocal in our criticism of welfare 'reforms' and the neoliberal ideology – with its particular view of human nature – upon which they are based. We need to challenge the idea that unemployment is a failure of the individual, and that vulnerable people should be forced into insecure, unpaid labour in order to receive state benefits. As a profession, we need to refuse to be the instruments of current policy in job centres and immigration detention centres, because to do so is to be complicit in human rights violations (R. Campbell, 2017; Jones, Wilson, Jarett, Kennedy, & Powell, 2017).

There are some who say that we can carry out this work and remain 'neutral'; that as professionals we can simply do our jobs and avoid 'taking sides'. In the current context, we do not believe this is possible. To work in settings such as these is to tacitly agree with the policies and ideologies embedded within those settings. We believe that, by doing so, one is automatically choosing a side, and that, in this context, at least, silence in the face of oppression puts us very much on the side of the oppressor. We have privileged knowledge as a result both of our training and, especially, of our daily conversations with service users. We need to use that knowledge to critique harmful policies and to offer psychologically informed alternatives. Refusing to be the agents of harmful policies is very different from neglecting to engage with policymakers in a more proactive way.

Improving services

As noted, the majority of us work in clinical settings, and, here too, we can apply our knowledge to improve services. We have discussed the limited provision of psychological therapy in statutory services, and there is a very clear argument to be made for increasing that provision. It is not necessarily the case, though, that the answer lies in just employing more psychologists. For example, crisis houses offer an effective and less coercive alternative to acute psychiatric wards (McNicholas, Rose, & Cooke, in prep.; Paton et al., 2016; Cooke, 2015), but these services do not necessarily need to be led by psychologists. Indeed, the most useful role for psychologists can often be supporting service user or survivor-led initiatives (e.g., Russo & Sweeney, 2016).

Involvement in service redesign and tendering is rarely offered to people early on in their careers, but it is perfectly possible to improve services in more subtle ways. Challenging discourses about 'suitability' for therapeutic work, promoting formulation as a means of understanding distress, and calling out institutional prejudice are all political acts. At the very least, we should be questioning and critiquing all instances of unethical and abusive practice, including for example, the inappropriate use of restraint on psychiatric wards. Of particular importance is to argue for a formulation-based, flexible approach to therapy provision rather than the diagnosis- and protocol-driven, time-limited cognitive-behaviour therapy which is, as noted earlier, sometimes all that is on offer (Leichsenring & Steinert, 2017).

Many of the people we work with will have had multiple adverse experiences and often have complex social and healthcare needs. We know that we are frequently unable to meet people's needs because we are working within a context which tries to pretend that that complexity doesn't exist. Our role, then, is to keep reminding the people who work in, run and pay for services that it does.

Sharing psychological thinking

Thanks to the democratisation of media – particularly since the popularisation of social media platforms – we also have real potential to bring psychological ideas into the mainstream to combat prejudice and discrimination. Whether or not we choose to engage in it, there is an ongoing public debate about the causes of mental health difficulties, about the 'treatments' that are helpful and unhelpful, and about the way society values those of us with mental health problems. A recent review found that much media coverage still promotes unhelpful stereotypes about people with mental health problems being victims of tragic diseases that make them strange and potentially violent (Rhydderch et al., 2016).

To misquote Edmund Burke, for unhelpful stereotypes to flourish requires only that those who know better to keep quiet. There is no impediment whatsoever to professionals (including those in training) providing a counter-narrative, whether by means of letters to editors, blogging, pitching comment articles or offering insights on phone-in radio programmes. The BPS media office (presscentre@bps. org.uk) holds a list of members who are willing to speak to journalists, though it is wise to be prepared for the rapid deadlines to which journalists often work. We both have experience of engaging in these forms of media, pre- and post-qualification, and wholeheartedly encourage our colleagues to build a media profile.

Interestingly, for one of us, being on the BPS media list has never resulted in any requests from journalists. In fact, almost all requests have initially come via social media channels (either Twitter or contact via blogs we write). As a rule, if you undertake media work your details will be kept on file and you may then be invited to contribute to discussions on a wide range of topics, though these requests tend to occur at irregular intervals. For those who would prefer to dip their toe into the water before offering to speak to the press, we have both found that social media – including Twitter, Facebook and blogging – can be excellent places to build networks, to learn and to mobilise.

Engaging in research

Similarly, we should use our scientific training to engage in emancipatory research, i.e., research which seeks to be of benefit to disadvantaged people (Noel, 2016) and to empower the subjects of social enquiry (Jupp, 2006). Too few of us continue to conduct research after qualifying (Newnes, 2014), but research is one of the most effective ways of demonstrating need, and although there are problems with the academic publishing model (Naughton, 2012), we should not view conducting research as an optional extra. Given the impact of early adversity on later outcomes, we could put our skills to good use by considering ways of reducing it both on a society-wide level and by means of individual early identification and intervention.

Working collaboratively

To achieve real change we need to work together. We must ensure that our professional bodies speak out and, where possible, take action on these issues, as well as supporting members to do so. As individuals, we need to encourage training programmes to include these topics as part of training, and to offer to be involved. We also need to get out of our clinical psychology 'silo', remember that we are a relatively small profession and collaborate with the many service users, survivors, social workers, counselling psychologists, psychiatrists and psychotherapists who are engaged in this work (Cutts, 2013; Priebe, 2015).

At pre-qualification level, there is ample opportunity to use university psychology societies and assistant psychologist groups to discuss the socio-political context of current policies and to consider how to promote social justice. There may also be opportunities to share some of these thoughts with organisations led by service users, and to collaborate on research or other projects. Assistant psychologists can bring these ideas to supervision – which, after all, is about developing you as a psychological thinker and practitioner, not just as a clinician. It may be the case that supervisors will have little knowledge of this area, but that need not be a barrier. The perspectives brought by pre-qualified colleagues are vital, and in our experience supervisors are often very willing to explore areas of debate that they are unfamiliar with.

Finally, we must collaborate with the people who use our services and who have found them wanting. A commitment to social justice must be founded on more than just good intentions. It must be based on real collaboration, in which the voices of the marginalised are privileged. 'Service user involvement' may be in vogue, but the truth is that professionals often co-opt real service user involvement to serve themselves. Sometimes, we need to step back, make space for others to speak and allow their voices to be privileged above our own.

Challenges to consider

So what are the challenges? Well, as we alluded to earlier, the scale of the task is vast, and change will come slowly. Although everyone has a part to play, seniority often brings the opportunity to make the most impact. The danger is that eager, socially aware young professionals who decide to go 'beyond therapy' can become disillusioned with the sheer enormity of the problems and, in some cases, burn out. This is why it is vital to have a network of people with whom you can plan and organise, but also seek support and exchange ideas. Although it is true that not all clinical psychologists are interested in activism, we know from our own experiences that, amongst those who are, close and rewarding friendships are often formed. And sometimes, when the task seems too great, it is likely to be those relationships which sustain you. We all need a sense of belonging, and activism is no exception.

We acknowledge that some readers will lack the confidence to engage in this work. In our view, there are two ways to build confidence: firstly to join with others as we have just described, and secondly to just do it, and keep doing it. Even if you get things wrong, you will learn, and you will do it better the next time.

Ultimately, though, it is vital to remember that – whatever our backgrounds – our professional qualification affords us much power and privilege. Having personal experience of social exclusion, poverty or discrimination may give us useful insights, but as clinical psychologists we need to acknowledge that we will view both our own and others' experiences a through a lens of professional privilege. We need to take care that our narratives do not drown out the stories of those who do not have the societal status we have acquired. Being allies should always be about the people we are allied with: not about us.

Conclusion

We began this chapter with a question, and we have tried to answer that question in the most emphatic terms. What we have written here is in some ways a manifesto, but it is a manifesto which has taken into account the views of both our fellow professionals and, more importantly, the people who use or who have survived the psychiatric system (we are particularly grateful to those people who responded to our requests for ideas for this chapter via social media; Cooke, 2018; Rahim, 2018). As clinical psychologists we are all, simply by doing our jobs, being political. We believe that we should be making our political choices in a more conscious way. We need to be aware of the extent to which we prop up harmful systems, and the extent to which we serve our own interests rather than those of the people who use our services. Our profession must make an active choice to change that. But our methods have to be guided – always – by those who are directly affected by our actions, and who bear the brunt of our (clinical psychology's and clinical psychologists') inaction.

Suggested further reading

Fernando, S. (2017). *Institutional racism in psychiatry and clinical psychology: Race matters in mental health.* London: Palgrave Macmillan.

Rogers, A., & Pilgrim, D. (2003). *Mental health and inequality*. Basingstoke: Palgrave MacMillan.

Smail, D. (2005). *Power, interest and psychology: Elements of a social materialist understanding of distress*. London: PCCS Books.

References

Barry, M., & Jenkins, R. (2007). *Implementing mental health promotion* (1st ed.). Philadelphia, PA: Elsevier Health Services.

Beyond the Therapy Room. (2017). *Beyond the therapy room*. Retrieved from www.psychologyfringe.com/speakers-2017/

Campbell, D. (2017, June 29). *NHS prescribed record number of antidepressants last year*. Retrieved from www.theguardian.com/society/2017/jun/29/nhs-prescribed-record-number-of-antidepressants-last-year

Campbell, R. (2017). *Locked up, locked out: Health and human rights in immigration detention*. London: British Medical Association.

Cooke, A. (1999). Clinical psychology, mental illness and the media. *Clinical Psychology Forum, 128*, 7–10.

Cooke, A. (2015). *'I'd rather die than go back to hospital': Why we need a non-medical crisis house in every town*. Retrieved from www.madinamerica.com/2015/10/id-rather-die-than-go-back-to-hospital-why-we-need-a-non-medical-crisis-house-in-every-town/

Cooke, A. (2018, January 29). I'm writing something with @MasumaRahim about how clinical psychologists need to be political. Any ideas/examples of political things that clinical psychologists do or should be doing? [Tweet]. Retrieved from https://twitter.com/AnneCooke14/status/958086631864627202

Cooke, A., Smythe, W., & Anscombe, P. (submitted). Conflict, compromise and collusion: Dilemmas for clinical psychologists in the mental health system. *Clinical Psychology & Psychotherapy*.

Cooper, K. (2018). *The devastating cost of treatment delays*. Retrieved from www.bma.org.uk/news/2018/february/the-devastating-cost-of-treatment-delays

Cutts, L. A. (2013). *Social justice in UK counselling psychology: Exploring the perspectives' of members of the profession who have a high interest in and commitment to social justice*. Manchester: University of Manchester.

Evans-Lacko, S., Corker, E., Williams, P., Henderson, C., & Thornicroft, G. (2014). Effect of the *Time to Change* anti-stigma campaign on trends in mental-illness-related public stigma among the English population in 2003–13: An analysis of survey data. *The Lancet Psychiatry, 1*(2), 121–128. doi:10.1016/S2215-0366(14)70243-3

Felitti, V. J., Anda, R. F., Nordenberg, D., Williamson, D. F., Spitz, A. M., Edwards, V., . . . Marks, J. S. (1998). Relationship of childhood abuse and household dysfunction to many of the leading causes of death in adults: The adverse childhood experiences (ACE) study. *American Journal of Preventive Medicine, 14*(4), 245–258. doi:10.1016/S0749-3797(98)00017-8

Fernando, S. (2017). *Institutional racism in psychiatry and clinical psychology: Race matters in mental health*. London: Palgrave Macmillan.

Fitch, C., Hamilton, S., Bassett, P., & Davey, R. (2011). The relationship between personal debt and mental health: A systematic review. *Mental Health Review Journal, 16*(4), 153–166. doi:10.1108/13619321111202313

Friedli, L. (2009). *Mental health, resilience and inequalities*. Copenhagen: World Health Organization.

Harper, D. (2016). Beyond individual therapy: Towards a psychosocial approach to public mental health. *The Psychologist, 29*, 440–444.

Ilyas, S., & Moncrieff, J. (2012). Trends in prescriptions and costs of drugs for mental disorders in England, 1998–2010. *The British Journal of Psychiatry, 200*(5), 393–398. doi:10.1192/bjp.bp.111.104257

Jones, A., Wilson, W., Jarett, T., Kennedy, S., & Powell, A. (2017). *The UN inquiry into the rights of persons with disabilities in the UK* (Report No. 07367). London: House of Commons Library.

Jupp, V. (2006). *The SAGE dictionary of social research methods*. London: Sage.

Leichsenring, F., & Steinert, C. (2017). Is cognitive behavioral therapy the gold standard for psychotherapy? The need for plurality in treatment and research. *Journal of American Medical Association, 318*(14), 1323–1324. doi:10.1001/jama.2017.13737

Longwill, A. (2015). *Clinical psychology workforce survey*. London: British Psychological Society.

McNicholas, S., Rose, A., & Cooke, A. (in prep.). Women and power: Drayton Park Women's Crisis House. In G. Sidley (Ed.), *Inside-out, outside-in: Alternatives to mainstream mental health services*. Ross-on-Wye, UK: PCCS Books.

Mental Health Foundation. (2016). *Fundamental facts about mental health*. London: Mental Health Foundation.

Mental Health Taskforce. (2016). *The five year forward view for mental health*. London: NHS England.

Murali, V., & Oyebode, F. (2004). Poverty, social inequality and mental health. *Advances in Psychiatric Treatment, 10*(3), 216–224. doi:10.1192/apt.10.3.216

Naughton, J. (2012, April 22). *Academic publishing doesn't add up*. Retrieved from www.theguardian.com/technology/2012/apr/22/academic-publishing-monopoly-challenged

Newnes, C. (2014). *Clinical psychology: A critical examination*. Ross-on-Wye, UK: PCCS Books.

Noel, L.-A. (2016). *Promoting an emancipatory research paradigm in design education and practice*. Paper presented at the Design Research Society 50th Anniversary Conference, Brighton, UK.

Paton, F., Wright, K., Ayre, N., Dare, C., Johnson, S., Lloyd-Evans, B., . . . Meader, N. (2016). Improving outcomes for people in mental health crisis: A rapid synthesis of the evidence for available models of care. *Health Technology Assessment, 20*(3), 1–162. doi:10.3310/hta20030

Priebe, S. (2015). The political mission of psychiatry. *World Psychiatry, 14*(1), 1–2. doi:10.1002/wps.20172

Rahim, M. (2014). Developmental trauma disorder: An attachment-based perspective. *Clinical Child Psychology and Psychiatry, 19*(4), 548–560. doi:10.1177/1359104514534947

Rahim, M. (2017). Social justice and equality: Preparing the next generations of psychologists to act. *Clinical Psychology Forum, 299*, 29–33.

Rahim, M. (2018). Folks, Anne Cooke and I are crowdsourcing via Twitter. May we do so here too? It's for a book chapter [Facebook]. Retrieved from www.facebook.com/photo.php?fbid=10100710279517960&set=gm.1716946765011587&type=3&theater

Rhydderch, D., Krooupa, A.-M., Shefer, G., Goulden, R., Williams, P., Thornicroft, A., . . . Henderson, C. (2016). Changes in newspaper coverage of mental illness from 2008 to 2014 in England. *Acta Psychiatrica Scandinavica, 134*, 45–52. doi: https://dx.doi.org/10.1111/acps.12606

Rogers, A., & Pilgrim, D. (2014). *A sociology of mental health and illness* (5th ed.). Maidenhead, UK: Open University Press.

Russo, J., & Sweeney, A. (Eds.). (2016). *Searching for a rose garden: Challenging psychiatry, fostering mad studies*. Ross-on-Wye, UK: PCCS Books.

Sharac, J., Mccrone, P., Clement, S., & Thornicroft, G. (2010). The economic impact of mental health stigma and discrimination: A systematic review. *Epidemiology and Psychiatric Sciences, 19*(3), 223–232. doi:10.1017/S1121189X00001159

Part III

Developing a professional identity as a clinical psychologist

Integrating the personal and professional

Chapter 11

A trainee's evolving experience of working collaboratively

Helen Walls

Summary points

- Working in a truly collaborative way is challenging and requires skill, confidence and reflection on one's own practice to ensure that clients are given as much choice as is possible in any therapeutic interaction.
- Our professional identity develops over training as we learn to work collaboratively with people towards positive therapeutic outcomes.
- Collaborative practice must take an integrative and adaptable approach to assessment and intervention, drawing on a range of theoretical frameworks, so that the individual needs of clients can be met accordingly.

The process of collaboration

Collaboration is defined as the mutual involvement of client and therapist in a helping relationship (Tryon & Winograd, 2011), which many factors can contribute to (Kazantzis & Kellis, 2012). Throughout training, I was acutely aware of the importance of collaborative practice and its role in psychological formulation and therapy (British Psychological Society; BPS, 2011). However, how I work collaboratively with clients has changed over time as my practice has evolved.

The process of working collaboratively with people, families and groups can arguably have two different meanings when it comes to thinking about what approach is used within psychological therapy. Both are centred on facilitating a warm, supportive, safe and containing relationship where the therapist listens to the person's story and is open to hearing his/her views, regularly checks his/her understanding and maintains transparency at all times. This process can then either;

(1) Become the basis to inform the therapist's approach to therapy.
(2) Prompt the engagement in joint decision-making with the client, with the therapist adapting his/her approach accordingly to fit with what the client wants.

This difference is subtle but significant; I felt that, as I progressed through training and my professional identity as a clinical psychologist begun to form, my therapeutic stance shifted to become more flexible and integrative, enabling me to match my approach to the unique needs of the client.

My approach

In the early stages of training, I believe I possessed some of the skills to facilitate the basis for working collaboratively with clients, such as providing a supportive and containing environment in sessions by engaging them in a warm and friendly manner and employing active listening skills: person-centred techniques based on Rogerian methods of human engagement (Rogers, 1951). These skills I perhaps already partly possessed, but they were developed during previous counselling skills courses I completed prior to training. Using person-centred techniques has the function of helping clients feel at ease in an unfamiliar situation and to feel heard and understood (see Tolan & Cameron, 2016, for a useful guide). Lambert and Barley (2002) refer to elements such as warmth, empathy, acceptance and therapeutic alliance as *common factors* in therapy, existing irrespective of the model being used. Horvath and Bedi (2002) define the alliance as "the quality and strength of the collaborative relationship between client and therapist, inclusive of mutual trust, liking, respect, and a sense of partnership" (p. 41).

While employing this approach, I was mindful of maintaining appropriate boundaries; warmth and empathy can have the potential to be misconstrued and it is the therapist's responsibility to monitor this. This awareness is guided by the BPS Code of Ethics and Conduct which states that standards of personal boundaries must be maintained, including being mindful of self disclosure and its use (BPS, 2009).

To work collaboratively, it is also necessary to gain consent from clients before beginning work with them. This is considered another common factor in therapy (Lambert & Barley, 2002). The BPS state that informed consent must be obtained from clients and that they should "be given ample opportunity to understand the nature, purpose and consequences of engaging with professional services" (BPS, 2009, p. 12).

Although my early practice was consistent with this guidance, my understanding of the importance of consent increased over training. On reflection, I acknowledge that, on occasions, some of the valuable establishing sessions with clients were rushed through, both due to lack of confidence, and because I was unaware of the true importance of this in terms of collaborative working. To develop in this area, it was necessary to provide clients with a clearer explanation of my role both as a trainee and as a psychologist, including my limits as a therapist and what the clients' role was in their therapy. Giving the clients more information would have provided more transparency and thus made the consent they gave informed, thereby truly adhering to the BPS guidelines of giving clients ample opportunity to understand (BPS, 2005). Furthermore, adapting my pace to fit a client's would have facilitated a more co-operative relationship and further increased the collaborative approach.

One example to illustrate this is from my adult psychology placement where I had clear remit to use short-term cognitive-behavioural therapy (CBT) with a young woman, who had a complex history and lots of stress in her current living situation. Lack of experience at this point in training, along with self-imposed and service pressures, caused me to rush into the therapy and work rigidly to my own agenda, holding fast to the CBT model I felt I was required to use. Unfortunately, little progress was made with this client in the time I had to work with her and a sound therapeutic alliance was not formed. Increasing my confidence has allowed me to trust the collaborative process and to feel comfortable working at a slower pace when required. Seeing clients respond well to this has helped me maintain this approach.

Alongside the need to hear the clients' views, it is also important to explore clients' goals and hopes for therapy. Often referred to as *goal consensus*, this is defined by Orlinsky, Grawe and Parks (1994) as the therapist-client agreement on therapy goals and expectations. Norcross (2011) cites this as being crucial for the development of the therapeutic relationship. Although efforts were made to establish goals with clients early on in my training, I believe I unintentionally took an *expert* role at times, suggesting directions for therapy that satisfied my agenda or ideas, rather than being genuinely guided by the client. Supervision and feedback from a reflective assignment allowed me to notice this and consider why I might be working in this way. It was useful to reflect on the power dynamics that exist in a therapeutic relationship; for example, clients may feel inferior or disempowered when accessing services for a number of reasons: therapists' high level of qualifications and professional status, level of knowledge of the therapist, lengthy waiting lists and often fighting to get seen by a service meaning they are lucky to be there and service pressures which limit number of sessions which may feel didactic, inflexible and imposed, etc. Through reflecting on this, I gradually developed my approach to be more responsive to a client's needs.

Models of therapy

In terms of models of therapy for intervention, there have also been some significant changes in my practice. My work with clients in early placements involved using specific models within formulation and therapy, which was predominantly informed by the supervisor's preferred way of working. I accepted this method of working as I lacked autonomy and confidence in my own decisions, but I have since recognised that I did not take a critical stance. For example, when a particular supervisor requested me to work within a CBT model with a client with low mood, I did so diligently, letting her guide me through the recommended model, but failed to consider alternative approaches and reflect with my supervisor on other methods to work with the client that may have benefited their progress further. My confidence restricted me in critiquing the chosen method and I was less thoughtful about my approach compared to how I now practice. Furthermore, my level of experience and knowledge to make some decisions meant I had to acknowledge my personal limits, which the Health and Care Professions Council (HCPC) states as one of the standards of conduct, performance and ethics for clinical psychologists to adhere to (HCPC, 2012).

I continued to use my engagement skills to develop a good working relationship with the client, which in part fitted with my desire to use a collaborative approach. For example, I worked jointly with the clients to understand their difficulties, used exploratory language, co-developed goals, agendas and formulations and amended these at clients' discretion, and employed *Socratic questioning* to guide the clients to their own answers, rather than impose my own thoughts upon them.

However, on reflection I acknowledge that my practice at this stage of training often involved fitting a client to the model of choice of the supervisor/service and to the evidence base, rather than tailoring and combining models in a more integrative way to fit a client's needs. This may have been appropriate for some clients' formulations, but the approach was not truly collaborative because there was no choice for the client over the type of therapy he/she engaged in. The BPS Professional Practice Guidelines (2017) assert that the client has a right to choose whether to receive psychological services, and moreover, to make this choice on the basis of the best information available. With the client mentioned earlier, a CBT approach would have been truly collaborative if she had been given a choice of approaches to work with, and had then made an informed decision about her therapy.

It is important to note here that this choice of therapeutic model is perhaps more specific to clinical psychologists rather than therapists in general. Clinical psychologists are trained in a range of therapeutic models and thus have the skills to work in an integrative way, according to client need. This suits the complex and often longstanding difficulties that clients who see clinical psychologists present with. However, in many primary care or Improving Access to Psychological Therapy (IAPT) services, who typically work with people with mild to moderate mental health problems, CBT is often the only approach staff are trained in and it may not be possible for clients to be given much choice. Depending on the organisational setup of the service, people may be offered CBT-based interventions first and then may experience a long wait for other approaches that might help.

Importantly, the choice of approach used within any psychological therapy is also guided by the ever-growing evidence base. Guidance from the National Institute for Health and Clinical Excellence (NICE) specifies that CBT should be used as a first line psychological intervention for common mental health problems including depression, anxiety, panic disorder, obsessive-compulsive disorder and post-traumatic stress disorder (NICE, 2011). The commissioning guide for the use of CBT (NICE, 2008) details advantages of using this approach such as efficacy, financial efficiency and relatively short treatment duration, while also briefly acknowledging the role of other therapies. Interestingly, however, it has been suggested that researchers have conducted roughly 75% of psychotherapy randomized control trials (RCTs) on CBT, meaning that realistic comparisons between different therapy modalities are rarely made (O'Donohue, Buchanan, & Fisher, 2000).

However, while the BPS acknowledge the value of single-model working in their Good Practice Guidelines on the use of Psychological Formulation document, they suggest that the fullest use of a clinical psychologist's skills would involve adopting a broad, integrated, multi-model perspective, taking into account a wide range of factors to understand a client's difficulties (BPS, 2011). Likewise, the Division of Clinical Psychology (DCP) state that clinical psychologists should be able to draw on a range of different models as necessary (DCP, 2010). I value the fact that we have this flexibility as clinical psychologists, but working in this way requires confidence and experience.

In terms of my development in this area, supervision was utilised to reflect on my practice tentatively. As the placements progressed, I begun to question the approaches being used; I considered how truly collaborative uni-modal ways of working are and wondered about how to work in a more integrative way. As my knowledge of psychological models and methods of working with clients developed, I became more confident in my abilities to work therapeutically and draw on a range of psychological models when working with a client to formulate his/her difficulties.

For example, a piece of work with a client involved co-developing a formulation of their current difficulties, which was informed by attachment models, behavioural principles, cognitive-behavioural theory and narrative approaches. We considered his relationship with his mother and her reluctance to allow him more independence, how his behaviour and mood were reinforced by the care he received, negative thoughts he frequently experienced in relation to himself, thus affecting his self-esteem, and also his identity as someone with a learning disability. We discussed different options he had about what he would like to work on and which techniques he might like to work with. This felt open and transparent, and gave the client choice, informed by my knowledge of psychological theory.

I also spent time reflecting on my practice during supervision and discussing how my professional identity is developing. This movement is something that Glaser and Strauss (1971) refer to as *status passage*. Although there is a paucity of literature around trainees' development of a professional identity, some authors have suggested that our beliefs about knowledge and uncertainty change as professional identity forms (e.g., Lingard, Garwood, Schryer, & Spafford, 2003). In the early stages of identity development, focus is given to the limitations of one's knowledge; what one cannot do or know. In the later stages of identity formation, knowledge is seen as evolving and dependent on context, and some acknowledgement is given to the fact that knowledge will always be developing (Lingard et al., 2003).

Although I was still guided by my supervisor in the later stages of training, I was more confident in making suggestions, questioning advice and thinking for myself about the appropriateness of the approach I might use with a particular client. I felt more able to offer clients a choice for how we could work together. I believe this was facilitated not only by having a supervisor who encouraged me to be a reflective practitioner, but also by experiencing a placement in a learning disabilities service that put great emphasis on equality and collaboration. The Government White Paper *Valuing People Now* (Department of Health, 2009) sets out four key principles when working with this population: rights, independent living, control and inclusion, which psychology services must embody in their approach. A more pronounced focus on human rights and joint working on through this placement helped me to recognise their importance, and become more competent in collaborative working.

On this placement, I worked with a middle-aged man with a diagnosis of a learning disability, who was also seeking a diagnosis of Autistic Spectrum Disorder (ASD). He had already been assessed for ASD and not given such a diagnosis, but he had become attached to services supporting him and continued to seek contact. Sadly, the gentleman had a negative reputation amongst many of the local services due to this level of attachment and dependence. I wondered if he was perhaps not being given the support he required due to this negative narrative. With the support of my supervisor, I used a person-centred approach and arranged a multidisciplinary meeting which the gentleman was invited to. I modelled collaboration and respect of the individual to work towards a shared goal which everyone was in agreement with.

Through this process of developing my professional identity as a clinical psychologist, I believe I now work in a way that reflects the second description of collaborative working outlined earlier – joint decision-making with the client and adaptability of the therapist. I have developed a strong awareness of power differentials that exist and work hard to minimise these. By virtue of training and experience, a clinical psychologist may have ideas about what might be a good approach to try; yet it is important to balance this with a client-centred position that fosters choice, ownership and independence.

Indeed, a collaborative decision-making framework could be considered to fit with Norcross's (2011) common factors for therapy. His extensive research would suggest that the model of therapy is not the most important consideration; decades of research suggest that the therapeutic relationship and the contribution of the client are the most robust predictors of treatment success. Lambert and Barley (2002) summarised 30 years of research to suggest that common factors such as warmth, empathy, confidentiality and therapeutic alliance were twice as likely to predict positive outcomes in therapy than specific therapy techniques. Earlier meta-analyses showing a strong link between therapeutic alliance and outcome of therapy had similar findings (Horvath & Symonds, 1991; Martin, Garske, & Davis 2000). Although studies relied primarily on self-reported data, these outcomes do offer support to the notion that the collaborative alliance is integral in the change process for the client (Bordin, 1979).

Conclusion

In conclusion, for practice to be considered truly collaborative, I believe it must principally involve the common factors on which Norcross (2011) places great importance. Collaborative practice must take an integrative and adaptable approach to assessment and intervention so that individual needs of clients can be met accordingly. Finally, it must give choice to the client, so that he/she can contribute and maintain a position of power in the relationship, and in his/her own psychological therapy. Combined with the therapist's knowledge, this should serve to balance the power between client and therapist, so that it is shared, not owned by one or the other. My developmental journey will continue to progress as a qualified clinical psychologist, and I look forward to ongoing formation of new opinions in this important area of professional practice.

Suggested further reading

Kazantzis, N., & Kellis, E. (2012). A special feature on collaboration in psychotherapy. *Journal of Clinical Psychology*, *68*(2), 133–135. doi:10.1002/jclp.21837

Norcross, J. C. (2011). *Psychotherapy relationships that work: Evidence-based responsiveness* (2nd ed.). New York, NY: Oxford University Press.

Tolan, J., & Cameron, R. (2016). *Skills in person-centred counselling & psychotherapy* (3rd ed.). London: Sage Publications Ltd.

References

Bordin, E. S. (1979). The generalizability of the psychoanalytic concept of the working alliance. *Psychotherapy: Theory, Research & Practice*, *16*(3), 252–260. doi:10.1037/h0085885

British Psychological Society. (2005). *Professional practice guidelines*. Leicester: BPS. Retrieved from www.bps.org.uk/sites/default/files/documents/professional_practice_guidelines_-_division_of_clinical_psychology.pdf

British Psychological Society. (2009). *Code of ethics and conduct*. Leicester: BPS. Retrieved from www.bps.org.uk/system/files/documents/code_of_ethics_and_conduct.pdf

British Psychological Society. (2011). *Good practice guidelines on the use of psychological formulation*. Leicester: BPS. Retrieved from www.canterbury.ac.uk/social-applied-sciences/ASPD/documents/DCPGuidelinesforformulation2011.pdf

British Psychological Society. (2017). *Professional practice guidelines* (3rd ed.). Leicester: BPS. Retrieved from www.bps.org.uk/sites/beta.bps.org.uk/files/Policy%20-%20Files/BPS%20Practice%20Guidelines%20(Third%20Edition).pdf

Department of Health. (2009). *Valuing people now. A new three-year strategy for people with learning disabilities – Making it happen for everyone*. Retrieved from http://webarchive.nationalarchives.gov.uk/20130105064234/www.dh.gov.uk/prod_consum_dh/groups/dh_digitalassets/documents/digitalasset/dh_093375.pdf

Division of Clinical Psychology. (2010). *Clinical psychology: The core purpose and philosophy of the profession*. Leicester: British Psychological Society.

Glaser, B. G., & Strauss, A. L. (1971). *Status passage*. London: Routledge and Kegan Paul Ltd.

Health and Care Professions Council. (2012). *Standards of conduct, performance and ethics*. Retrieved from www.hcpc-uk.org/assets/documents/10003B6EStandardsofconduct,performanceandethics.pdf

Horvath, A. O., & Bedi, R. P. (2002). The alliance. In J. C. Norcross (Ed.), *Psychotherapy relationships that work: Therapist contributions and responsiveness to patients* (pp. 37–69). New York, NY: Oxford University Press.

Horvath, A. O., & Symonds, B. D. (1991). Relation between working alliance and outcome in psychotherapy: A meta-analysis. *Journal of Counseling Psychology, 38*(2), 139–149. doi:10.1037/0022-0167.38.2.139

Kazantzis, N., & Kellis, E. (2012). A special feature on collaboration in psychotherapy. *Journal of Clinical Psychology, 68*(2), 133–135. doi:10.1002/jclp.21837

Lambert, M. J., & Barley, D. E. (2002). Research summary on the therapeutic relationship and psychotherapy outcome. In J. C. Norcross (Ed.), *Psychotherapy relationships that work: Therapist contributions and responsiveness to patients* (pp. 17–32). New York, NY: Oxford University Press.

Lingard, L., Garwood, K., Schryer, C. F., & Spafford, M. M. (2003). A certain art of uncertainty: Case presentation and the development of professional identity. *Social Science & Medicine, 56*(3), 603–616. doi:10.1016/s0277-9536(02)00057-6

Martin, D. J., Garske, J. P., & Davis, M. K. (2000). Relation of the therapeutic alliance with outcome and other variables: A meta-analytic review. *Journal of Consulting and Clinical Psychology, 68*(3), 438–450. doi:10.1037/0022-006X.68.3.438

National Institute for Health and Clinical Excellence. (2008). *Common mental health disorders: Identification and pathways to care.* London: National Institute for Health and Clinical Excellence.

National Institute for Health and Clinical Excellence. (2011). *Cognitive behavioural therapy for the management of common mental health problems: Commissioning guide.* London: National Institute for Health and Clinical Excellence.

Norcross, J. C. (2011). *Psychotherapy relationships that work: Evidence-based responsiveness* (2nd ed.). New York, NY: Oxford University Press.

O'Donohue, W., Buchanan, J. A., & Fisher, J. E. (2000). Characteristics of empirically supported treatments. *Journal of Psychotherapy Practice and Research, 9*(2), 69–74. Retrieved from http://vuir.vu.edu.au/19368/29/00jpr069.pdf

Orlinsky, D. E., Grawe, K., & Parks, B. (1994). Process and outcome in psychotherapy-Noch einmal. In A. E. Bergin & S. L. Garfield (Eds.), *Handbook of psychotherapy and behaviour change* (4th ed., pp. 270–378). New York, NY: Wiley.

Rogers, C. (1951). *Client-centered therapy: Its current practice, implications and theory.* London: Constable & Robinson.

Tolan, J., & Cameron, R. (2016). *Skills in person-centred counselling & psychotherapy* (3rd ed.). London: Sage Publications Ltd.

Tryon, G. S., & Winograd, G. (2011). Goal consensus and collaboration. In J. C. Norcross (Ed.), *psychotherapy relationships that work: Evidence-based responsiveness* (2nd ed., pp. 109–125). New York, NY: Oxford University Press.

Chapter 12

Self-disclosure as a therapeutic tool

Ethical and practical considerations

Sarah Davidson

Summary points

- The issue of therapist self-disclosure is complex and has been the subject of much debate in the literature.
- A number of ethical and professional issues need to be considered when contemplating the use of therapist self-disclosure.
- As part of developing a strong and healthy sense of professional identity, practitioners should make good use of supervision, be aware of professional guidelines and reflect on the individual characteristics of each case prior to making any kind of self-disclosure.

What is self-disclosure?

Goldstein (1997) defines self-disclosure as "the therapist's conscious verbal behavioural sharing of thoughts, feelings, attitudes, interests, tastes, experiences, or factual information about himself or herself or about significant relationships and activities in the therapist's life" (p. 419). When developing a professional identity as a clinical psychologist, an issue which remains significant throughout our career is that of deciding what and how we share about ourselves with service users. The issue of self-disclosure is, of course, relevant for professionals in any role whose work involves developing a rapport with clients. As different disciplines may draw diverse conclusions when considering this issue, we should consider a range of literature sources when thinking about how this relates to clinical psychology practice.

In addition, modern-day internet technologies have resulted in clients now having hugely expanded access to personal information relating to their therapists, redefining the meaning and application of self-disclosure and transparency in therapy (Zur, Williams, Lehavot, & Knapp, 2009). It is now easy for people to find out professional and personal information about their psychologist before they even meet – a simple Facebook profile picture might give clues about someone's marital status, sexuality, hobbies, socioeconomic status, political leanings and so on. Factors such as these might have a significant impact on the therapeutic relationship. As clinical psychologists, we must make decisions about what we may or may not disclose within the confines of an individual therapy session, alongside considering how open we choose to be in our virtual lives.

Should we share information about ourselves?

In related professions such as substance misuse counselling, self-disclosure is regarded as an important skill (White, 2000). However, the idea of sharing information about oneself during clinical psychology training often creates a lot of anxiety. Clinical supervisors for trainees on placement may encourage or discourage this, depending on the nature of the service they work in and their own professional ideology. Self-disclosure can certainly create challenges and requires careful consideration; however it can create powerful opportunities within a therapeutic relationship if used to good clinical effect.

From my clinical experience, much of which has come from working with people with traumatic attachment histories (many of whom have spent lengthy periods in the criminal justice system), I believe that self-disclosure can be a powerful tool. The act of sharing small details with clients about my own life or experiences has had a profound impact in therapy. I have found that this has facilitated more meaningful engagement, on a human level, as part of a positive interaction. Such decisions always have to mitigated and balanced against a number of other factors, particularly where careful management of risk is required. Many of the people I have worked with have violent or aggressive histories, and some have developed unhealthy relationships with professionals which ultimately can cause harm to everyone involved. However, I would argue that careful and thoughtful use of self-disclosure can lead to a subsequent reduction in risk: for example, through helping a client to learn about appropriate boundaries within a trusting relationship.

Freud derided the use of self-disclosure in psychotherapy, recommending that it should be avoided at all costs (Freud, 2001). Freud may have started this discussion over 100 years ago, yet it continues to be a topic of some debate. Henretty and Levitt (2010) conducted a qualitative review of self-disclosure in psychotherapy, highlighting highly divergent results across the available research and a lack of clarity about the potential implications for clients. From the 24 reviewed studies which looked at the effect of self-disclosure on clients, 20 studies showed that therapists who used self-disclosures elicited more positive responses than those who did not (Henretty & Levitt, 2010). Other studies have shown that self-disclosure in therapy can help with building rapport, normalising client experiences, promoting client disclosure and autonomy and offering alternative ways of thinking or coping within a safe environment (e.g., Hanson, 2005; Edwards & Murdock, 1994; Audet, 2011). This certainly offers some empirical support to the suggestion that there are instances where self-disclosure can be beneficial.

However, such findings must be interpreted with caution. Goldstein's (1997) definition of self-disclosure seemingly suggests an almost innumerable number of options when considering what we might choose to share with our clients. Other researchers define self-disclosure in different ways, and this can become problematic when considering not only what practitioners consider a disclosure to be, but also interpreting research findings around the implications of such disclosure (Weiner, 1983). We must also consider the relevance of such research considering the breadth of clinical situations in which we work.

In terms of national guidance for clinical psychologists, the Health and Care Professions Council (HCPC) has produced two documents which provide ethical and professional guidelines applicable to the issue of self-disclosure. These guidelines are helpful starting point in beginning to think about the potential risks involved in self-disclosure. The Standards of Conduct, Performance and Ethics (HCPC, 2016) and Standards of Proficiency for Practitioner Psychologists (HCPC, 2015) highlight the importance of professional relationships and appropriately responsible use of communication (including social media websites). The guidance also discusses the complexity of relationships with service users and the inherent power imbalances within them; highlighting the importance of managing and maintaining appropriate boundaries. The British Psychological Society (2009) has also provided ethical guidelines which highlight how the relationship between psychologist and client is a powerful one, with the potential to be harmful and exploitative if not managed correctly.

What should I disclose?

The therapeutic orientation of a therapist can impact on the decision to use self-disclosure, and the reasons for doing so. Peterson (2002), Ham, Lemasson, and Hayes (2013) and Gibson (2012), all make reference to the ways in which therapeutic models can affect the way in which practitioners chose to use disclosure in therapy. Yalom (1985) stated "more than any other single characteristic, the nature and degree of therapist self-disclosure differentiates the various schools of . . . therapy" (p. 212).

This difference in perspective can vary greatly. Many traditional psychoanalytic therapists are strongly opposed to the use of any form of self-disclosure, believing that such disclosures may alter transference processes (Edwards & Murdock, 1994). Conversely, within a Humanistic approach to therapy the ability of the practitioner to be themselves freely is emphasised (Weiner, 1983). Contemporary clinical psychology training focuses on practicing in an integrated fashion, drawing on a range of therapeutic modalities to deliver high quality psychological intervention. This has the potential to make the decision to self-disclose more complex. The range of settings in which clinical psychologists work also impacts on this; for example, in forensic settings self-disclosure may be discouraged. Meanwhile, in relationally focused, progressive environments such as therapeutic communities the emphasis on interpersonal relationships means that the use of self-disclosure may be more common than in weekly one-to-one sessions within a traditional psychology service.

A lack of confidence in knowing when it is safe and appropriate to use self-disclosure is particularly common during clinical psychology training. Trainees are learning to navigate the complexities of clinical psychology practice, developing competencies in a range of approaches and working with a range of supervisors. Some trainees may feel that they want to utilise this tool early on, particularly if their own experiences have been especially significant to them. Others may feel it is an addition to their therapeutic repertoire that they only feel comfortable in trialling when they feel more established in their clinical practice. Whatever the level of experience and competence, appropriate and carefully guided supervision to facilitate reflection around such issues is key.

A review into self-disclosure from counsellors (Henretty, Currier, Berman, & Levitt, 2014) concluded that the most helpful disclosures were ones which revealed similarity between client and counsellor, were of negative content valence or were related to experiences either inside or outside the therapy. Exploring this in more detail, Ziv-Beiman, Keinan, Livneh, Malone and Shahar (2017) found that *immediate self-disclosure* (i.e., sharing feelings about the client or the relationship in the moment) reduced measurable levels of distress amongst clients and strengthened a favourable perception of the therapist, compared to when therapists made *non-immediate self-disclosure* (sharing information about the therapist's life outside the intervention) or no disclosures at all.

Henretty and Levitt (2010) also acknowledge the importance of timing when considering self-disclosure. They draw attention to the inconsistencies in the literature in relation to the point in therapy where this might be most useful. For example, Simon (1988) reports that therapists may choose to self-disclose early in therapy in order to build alliance and relieve apprehension, while Audet and Everall (2003) and Geller (2003) warn of the danger of using self-disclosure while clients are still becoming accustomed to the process of therapy. Of course, as outlined earlier, social media and online information may mean that clients may learn information about their therapist outside of the therapeutic space. There are no hard and fast rules here; each situation should be considered individually.

What can help the decision-making process?

In addition to the requirements set by regulatory bodies, Koocher and Keith-Spiegel (1998) suggest that clinical psychologists should adhere to nine principles when making a professional decision around an ethical dilemma. These principles could be relevant when thinking about self-disclosure, as they are based on the overall premise that psychologists should avoid doing harm to clients and aim to help or benefit them.

(1) Determine that the matter is an ethical one.
(2) Consult available guidelines that might apply to a specific identification and possible resolution.

(3) Consider, as best as possible, all sources that might influence the kind of decision you will make.
(4) Consult with a trusted colleague.
(5) Evaluate the rights, responsibilities and vulnerability of all affected parties.
(6) Generate alternative decisions.
(7) Enumerate the consequences of making each decision.
(8) Make the decision.
(9) Implement the decision.

(Koocher & Keith-Spiegel, 1998)

In addition, particular clients will elicit differing emotional responses in clinicians, which may or may not affect the decision to disclose. In forensic services, a useful model for observing our relationship with clients is Hamilton's *Boundary See Saw Model* (Hamilton, 2010). This model encourages reflection on where we sit on the continuum of the roles being adopted within an interaction: from being overly controlling to overly pacifying. The model advocates aiming for a middle position within which care can be provided which offers flexibility and responsiveness within explicit limits and boundaries. I have found this to be a useful relational tool in aiding the on-going decision-making process around whether to disclose information about myself or share my own experiences. Being able to reflect on roles and dynamics within clinical supervision has always helped me to take a step back and think about why I might be feeling tempted to make a disclosure – or why I might be avoiding doing so.

Disclosure and the development of a professional identity

During training we begin a journey of self-reflection and developing awareness that is as often uncomfortable as it is revelationary. Considering why we might choose to disclose information is one of the most important reflective processes we engage in, both individually and in our supervision (Peterson, 2002).

It would be unethical and in breach of HCPC (2016) professional guidelines for clinical psychologists to use self-disclosure as a means of meeting their own needs (Gutheil & Gabbard 1995). However, it can be difficult for a psychologist to genuinely take a mental step back and consider whether his/her self-disclosure is wholly for the therapeutic benefit of the client. Combined with the countertransference issues present in many (if not all) therapeutic interactions, this becomes a complex, multifaceted issue. Our ability to observe our own ethical practice is a constantly changing, dynamic process. Continued use of clinical supervision and reflective practice to attempt to eliminate, as far as possible, the unintended practice of self-disclosure for self-support purposes really is essential.

Echoing the thoughts of Henretty and Levitt (2010), it is also suggested that a greater emphasis be placed on this issue during clinical psychology training in order to better prepare trainees with the range of skills and sensitivity necessary to use this technique effectively, and provide them with a safe space to contemplate the issue more generally outside of therapy sessions. As Geller (2003) argues, teaching has the potential to provide: "the precepts, rules, criteria, and cognitive processes that guide effective clinical decision making relative to therapist self-disclosure" (p. 543, in Henretty & Levitt, 2010). For those currently undergoing clinical training or hoping to in the near future, I would encourage you to use this chapter as a starting point for thinking about how you will develop your professional identity around issues such as self-disclosure, and how this might influence your practice.

Conclusion

This chapter has considered the use self-disclosure as a therapeutic tool in the context of developing a professional identity. It is not realistic or helpful to aim for a static viewpoint on this topic; however this chapter has introduced some starting points for reflection. The multifaceted relationship between service user and clinical psychologist is unique in every instance, as is the blend of content of self-disclosure, reason for self-disclosure, therapeutic method and transference/countertransference. The decision to self-disclose or not should be made independently on every occasion, using a combination of clinical judgement, ethical and professional guidance and clinical supervision. This is a topic that may be particularly pertinent for those training in or working towards a career in clinical psychology; however pro-active reflection on issues around self-disclosure should be a career-long endeavour.

Suggested further reading

Danzer, G. S. (2018). *Therapist self-disclosure: An evidence-based guide for practitioners.* London: Routledge.

Derlaga, V. J., & Berg, J. H. (Eds.). (1987). *Self-disclosure: Theory, research, and therapy.* New York, NY: Springer.

Fisher, M., & Shueman, S. (Eds.). (1990). *Self-disclosure in the therapeutic relationship.* New York, NY: Springer.

References

Audet, C., & Everall, R. D. (2003). Counsellor self-disclosure: Client-informed implications for practice. *Counselling and Psychotherapy Research, 3*(3), 223–231. doi:10.1080/14733140312331384392

Audet, C. T. (2011). Client perspectives of therapist self-disclosure: Violating boundaries or removing barriers? *Counseling Psychology Quarterly, 24,* 85–100. doi:10.1080/14733140312331384392Edwards, C. E., & Murdock, N. L. (1994). Characteristics of therapist self-disclosure in the counseling process. *Journal of Counseling and Development, 72,* 384–389. doi:10.1002/j.1556-6676.1994.tb00954.x

Freud, S. (2001). Recommendations to physicians practising psycho-analysis. In J. Strachey (Ed. & Trans.), *The Standard edition of the psychological works of Sigmund Freud* (Vol. 12, pp. 1–120). London: Hogarth Press. (Original work published in 1912)

Geller, J. D. (2003). Self-disclosure in psychoanalytic – Existential therapy. *Journal of Clinical Psychology, 59*(5), 541–554. doi:10.1002/jclp.10158

Gibson, M. F. (2012). Opening up: Therapist self-disclosure in theory, research, and practice. *Clinical Social Work Journal, 40*(3), 287–296. doi:10.1007/s10615-012-0391-4

Goldstein, E. G. (1997). To tell or not to tell: The disclosure of events in the therapist's life to the patient. *Clinical Social Work Journal, 25*, 41–58. doi:10.1023/A:1025729826627

Gutheil, T. G., & Gabbard, G. O. (1995). The concept of boundaries in clinical practice: Theoretical and risk management dimensions. In D. N. Bersoff (Ed.), *Ethical conflicts in psychology* (pp. 218–223). Washington, DC: American Psychological Association.

Ham, C. C., LeMasson, K. D. S., & Hayes, J. A. (2013). The use of self-disclosure: Lived experiences of recovering substance abuse counselors. *Alcoholism Treatment Quarterly, 31*(3), 348–374. doi:10.1080/07347324.2013.800399

Hamilton, L. (2010). The Boundary Seesaw Model: Good fences make for good neighbours. In A. Tennant & K. Howells (Eds.), *Using time, not doing time: Practitioner perspectives on personality disorder and risk* (pp. 181–194). Chichester, UK: John Wiley & Sons Ltd.

Hanson, J. (2005). Should your lips be zipped? How therapist self-disclosure and non-disclosure affects clients. *Counselling and Psychotherapy Research, 5*(2), 96–104. doi:10.1080/17441690500226658

Health and Care Professions Council. (2015). *Standards of proficiency – Practitioner psychologists.* Retrieved from www.hcpc-uk.org/assets/documents/10002963SOP_Practitioner_psychologists.pdf

Health and Care Professions Council. (2016). *Standards of conduct, performance and ethics.* Retrieved from www.hcpc-uk.org/aboutregistration/standards/standardsofconductperformanceandethics/

Henretty, J. R., Currier, J. M., Berman, J. S., & Levitt, H. M. (2014). The impact of counsellor self-disclosure on clients: A meta-analytic review of experimental and quasi-experimental research. *Journal of Counseling Psychology, 61*, 191–207. doi:10.1037/a0036189

Henretty, J. R., & Levitt, H. M. (2010). The role of therapist self-disclosure in psychotherapy: A qualitative review. *Clinical Psychology Review, 30*(1), 63–77. doi:10.1016/j.cpr.2009.09.004

Koocher, G. P., & Keith-Spiegel, P. (1998). *Ethics in psychology: Professional standards and cases* (2nd ed.). New York, NY: Oxford University Press.

Peterson, Z. (2002). More than a mirror: The ethics of therapist self-disclosure. *Psychotherapy: Theory, Research, Practice, Training, 39*(1), 21–31. doi:10.1037/0033-3204.39.1.21

Simon, J. C. (1988). Criteria for therapist self-disclosure. *American Journal of Psychotherapy, 42*(3), 404–415. doi:10.1176/appi.psychotherapy.1988.42.3.404

Weiner, M. F. (1983). *Therapist disclosure: The use of self in psychotherapy* (2nd ed.). Baltimore, MD: University Park Press.

White, W. L. (2000). The history of recovered people as wounded healers: I. From native America to the rise of the modern alcoholism movement. *Alcoholism Treatment Quarterly, 18*(1), 1–23. doi:10.1300/J020v18n01_01

Yalom, I. D. (1985). *The theory and practice of group psychotherapy*. New York, NY: Basic Books.

Ziv-Beiman, S., Keinan, G., Livneh, E., Malone, P. S., & Shahar, G. (2017). Immediate therapist self-disclosure bolsters the effect of brief integrative psychotherapy on psychiatric symptoms and the perceptions of therapists: A randomized clinical trial. *Psychotherapy Research, 27*(5), 558–570. doi:10.1080/10503307.2016.1138334

Zur, O., Williams, M. H., Lehavot, K., & Knapp, S. (2009). Psychotherapist self-disclosure and transparency in the internet age. *Professional Psychology: Research and Practice, 40*(1), 22–30. doi:10.1037%2Fa0014745

Chapter 13

Through the looking glass

Reflections on the transition from a trainee to a qualified clinical psychologist

Liam Gilligan and Denise Herron

Summary points

- The supervisory relationship offers a useful perspective on the development of a professional identity, through the period of transition from trainee to qualified clinical psychologist.
- The wider NHS context and the organisational/political landscape is a major contributing factor in the development of a professional identity.
- Trainees should be supported to reflect on how these wider contextual factors impact the development of their professional identity, alongside more individual aspects of this including their values, past experiences and relationships with colleagues.

The development of a professional identity as a clinical psychologist is a constantly evolving process which occurs throughout a person's career. It cannot be separated from the ever-changing social and political context to which we find ourselves bound. The foundations of this developing professional identity are predominantly established during clinical training, during which there is the opportunity for trainees to immerse themselves in their new profession and safely begin to take on the responsibilities required of a qualified clinician under the guidance and supervision of a qualified clinical psychologist.

Supervision is regarded as essential in the professional development of clinical psychologists throughout their careers, with professional policy dictating that regardless of stage of career or work context, regular, planned supervision of work is required (British Psychological Society, 2014). While the primary purpose of supervision is to ensure safety and quality of care for service users through monitoring the supervisee's work, it also offers the opportunity to support a clinician's professional development, allowing a space to reflect on the personal impact of his/her work and the broader competencies in which they need to develop, while educating and guiding their general professional practice (British Psychological Society, 2014; O'Donovan, Halford, & Walters, 2011). Models of personal and professional development in clinical psychology have identified supervision as an essential element (O'Donovan et al., 2011). Within the context of this supervisory relationship, the authors will explore the development of professional identity in the transition from trainee clinical psychologist to qualified clinical psychologist.

Liam (LG) first approached Denise (DH) when he was a second-year trainee clinical psychologist at the University of East Anglia, enquiring about a possible specialist placement with her service in adult mental health, specifically focusing on therapy in complex and challenging presentations. Under the supervision of DH, LG was placed in a specialist team in Suffolk, created to work differently with patients who may struggle to engage with traditional mental health services. These groups primarily met the criteria for a diagnosis of personality disorder, longstanding psychosis or 'treatment resistant' mental health difficulties, with cases selected because they were complex or interpersonally challenging. After the completion of his training, LG then returned to the service to work in his first qualified clinical psychologist post. DH continued to offer clinical supervision. This presented an excellent opportunity to examine the development of a professional identity during the developmental period between trainee clinical psychologist and qualified clinical psychologist through the evolving supervisory relationship.

To explore these issues, the authors met and discussed how the change in their relationship throughout the transition was experienced, the challenges that emerged before and after it, and the personal impact of the process. The idea of professional development was held in mind alongside this. To identify the main themes of this conversation and provide a starting point for further reflection, thematic analysis (Braun & Clarke, 2006) was undertaken on the content of this discussion. Thematic analysis is a method of analysing qualitative data to identify specific patterns, known as 'themes'. These themes were then further explored and reflected on during the writing of this chapter.

Theme one: 'the impact of the system'

The strongest theme to emerge from the conversation was the impact of the system around the psychologists, specifically the NHS trust that they were both working in. Following a period of significant organisational change, the trust was placed in special measures twice by the Care Quality Commission who demanded an immediate improvement in the care they provide. This systemic pressure seemed to permeate multiple levels of the system, influencing professional development not only from a more localised, team-based perspective, but also from a wider organisational and political perspective. This was not a surprising reflection, given that training and work environments have been identified as a contextual factor for professional development in trainee clinical psychologists, with different levels of environmental stress, challenge or conduciveness to self-exploration hypothesised to impact on this development in different ways (Elman, Illfelder-Kaye, & Robiner, 2005).

Coming into the organisation at a time of radical change and restructure, LG joined a team based on a new model of service delivery for a client group often identified as complex and challenging. Both the team and the wider organisation were in a state of flux. Elements identified as requisite for a healthy organisation, namely clarity regarding primary task, structure, basic principles for delivery of service and regular space for reflection (Stokoe, 2011), were significantly lacking.

Within this demanding environment, there was an increased sense of responsibility along with being acutely aware of the team's expectations and LG's self-imposed pressure to 'prove himself':

DH: That's a real shift in terms of those beliefs and attitudes, where you were as a trainee, and I think more so towards the end of your placement, but particularly post-qualified, of that high level of responsibility that you have held or articulated for sorting out a team that's really struggling.

LG: . . . one of the frustrations I've had this year and it links very directly to the idea of professional identity is, that as we've lost staff I've had to pick up more generic work, more care coordination work, and, I've had less opportunity because of the constraints on me to do what you might typically see as clinical psychology work, and because of needs in the organisation, losing the ability and time to do some of the wider systemic stuff as well, facilitating groups or doing research or organisational work or service development. . . .

DH: you've been in a team where your professional identity has been eroded a lot, because of the needs of the team, and the things that you've been pulled into because of that.

As noted here, it was felt there was less opportunity for LG to develop a post-qualification identity specifically linked to clinical psychology in this team, due to the needs of the service changing what was required of a clinical psychologist. Assessment, formulation, supervision and treatment directly informed by psychological theory could not be prioritised, with the work instead becoming more generic and non-specific in nature. This was felt to be a direct consequence of the mounting service pressures of referrals and limited team capacity to manage the workload, and the subsequent detrimental impact this was having on the wellbeing of team members themselves. Consequently, psychological thinking and interventions were limited for both staff and patients, and the focus on generic work limited the development of skills specific to being a clinical psychologist.

Considering this within the wider political and economic landscape, a report by The Kings Fund (Gilburt, 2018) highlights the lack of parity of esteem for mental healthcare as opposed to physical healthcare, and the impact transforming care and cost reduction has had on recruitment and retention, safe delivery of services and staff wellbeing. This has been felt strongly by both authors, with LG referencing Gilbert's (2009) compassion-focused model to understand the organisation as one which was threat-focused and ready to attack or pull rank on the individuals within it:

LG: It's interesting that, as the NHS feels more under threat, as more teams and more structures are going to potentially be in that threat mode or very *responsive*, how is that going to have an impact on any clinical psychologist developing their qualified identity, and what do you need to put into place in order to protect that and safeguard that development?

It was within this wider organisational context that DH noted in particular how the experience of supervising LG felt different in comparison to other trainees and newly qualified psychologists. This may have been due to the preceptorship nature of LG's role, within which he was employed post-qualification in a temporary transitional role/pay banding, enabling him to consolidate and develop his skills as a practitioner with a clear path for progression to a higher band. This also highlighted how the changing face of the NHS cannot be underestimated as a key factor in professional identity formation:

DH: What's been different this time has definitely been the organisation and the NHS generally, in terms of the impact it has on us, our own wellbeing, our sense of identity within the organisation . . . how to move into a leadership role, a key part of that preceptorship . . . but leadership within a system that's under threat and has capacity issues. . . . I think the stuff around identity has been less clear, and I wonder if most professions might say that at the moment because of the issues around demand, and the way people have had to work more generically.

These reflections from DH mirrored the thoughts that LG had around development of identity within his team, noticing that those in the organisation with specialist jobs or skills had undertaken the more generic care co-ordination work that became the main focus of the role, because the demand for services had exceeded what could be provided. DH had noticed this shift in the topics staff were bringing to discuss in supervision with her, finding that this focus had moved to the process of managing service demands and discharge. This left less room for the elements of supervision which helped to shape a professional identity, such as a focus on specific skills and a clear space for the supervisee to explore who they are and what they want to be as a professional.

Theme two: 'transitional worries and fears'

As might be expected, much of the conversation centred around the fears and concerns that seemed to occur naturally as part of being a trainee, and the transition towards qualification. One element focused on how fear may have acted as a push factor towards an area of professional development in which the trainee felt vulnerable or ill equipped. In this case, this was about working with more complex, interpersonally challenging cases:

LG: My worry was that if I was going to be the only team psychologist, I wanted to feel confident and self-assured that I could handle those kinds of cases, that I was going to be able to manage on my own.

However, while self-reflection and understanding personal limitations is a crucial element of professional development, at this stage this was seen very much within a more naïve or training-focused mindset; of having something that needed to be completed in order to feel more prepared for qualified life. It was only through placement experience and the subsequent supervision that followed, that this could be explored more widely:

LG: it's that trainee mindset of having to tick something off . . . if I haven't done it in a placement I can't do it, and it's that, needing to tick that box or get that one little bit and I'll be absolutely fine as a psychologist.

DH: . . . and that sense that actually, you weren't just going to be able to do that, you know, give me this piece of work to do, teach me how to do it, I'll learn how and then I'll have done it . . . that sense of, I just need to get this sorted and then I'll be done. I remember that first supervision after you'd had that really difficult session, and the look of horror on your face!

LG's original push for this placement was understood to be linked at least in part to a sense of *imposter syndrome* (Clance & Imes, 1978), a concept characterised by persistent doubt in abilities or fear of being exposed as a fraud or incompetent:

LG: But hitting a lot of buttons around not being good enough . . . that imposter syndrome that gets very heavily identified in clinical psychology trainees . . . and really feeling, because I was a third year . . . at that point was preparing for professional life, for qualified life, and, those dynamics really hitting some of the inadequacies and the sense that, I might not be able to do this.

This term, while generally seen as a colloquial concept, is likely to be familiar to clinical psychologists who have moved through a training pathway in which competition, high standards and self-reflection can often encourage a strong sense of anxiety around whether they are *good enough*. This will influence the development of professional identity; there is no established, tangible metric of what a *good* psychologist should be like. How this sense of uncertainty is understood and managed by the trainee is of key importance to his/her ongoing professional development.

However, despite this period of anxiety and tension, reflecting on his position two years post-qualified, LG felt a sense of becoming more comfortable and established within his professional identity:

LG: It's interesting just thinking about myself as a trainee all those years ago, and where I am now, and I don't know, I definitely feel more self-assured, I definitely feel more able to be flexible and roll with things. . . .

DH: what I get a sense of now is someone who is, who doesn't talk about being an imposter anymore, I think you are OK with being a psychologist now, I think you have developed an identity as a psychologist. . . .

DH: I've seen you be much more confident at taking leadership . . . you had to deal with some really difficult leadership issues . . . and times when were not treated well, and I think that's been a learning curve for you . . . developing an identity where you want to be able to take a lead.

While there are likely to be many attributes which have allowed a more comfortable sense of professional identity to grow, the conversation identified that this seems to have developed alongside a move beyond a trainee mindset, with LG having a greater appreciation for what is required in the professional world outside of clinical training:

LG: I wanted this placement because I was concerned about myself and therefore how I as a single individual would have the right attributes, and it's interesting . . . my reflection there is seeing how far that has now widened and actually . . . to think more systemically, and consider the wider impact.

Alongside this, one attribute which cannot be overlooked in development of a more established professional sense of self, is the responsibility which comes from LG also becoming a supervisor himself, while still having to manage and confront some of the same anxieties and doubts that emerged:

DH: It's been nice to see you develop your confidence in having a trainee and I think that's been interesting because when we've done the joint supervision I think there's been a couple of times where you've doubted yourself again in relation to that, and I think that's been interesting about where that's taken you.

Theme three: 'the values and baggage that you bring'

One theme to emerge from the conversation was around the life experiences that the trainee brings to a placement and his/her wider training journey. LG reflected that he often felt uncomfortable within the world of clinical psychology, drawing upon his own personal experiences of having to decide whether to go into medicine as an alternative career:

DH: You articulated this clearly, you talked initially about am I in the right profession, am I more of a medic, you know, am I more this, am I in the right place?
LG: . . . and that a lot of that stuff as well, coming into the placement, is a lot of my own baggage and . . . feeling that I've never quite fitted or I've always been a bit of a square peg in a round hole in psychology and, yeah, I think being aware of the stuff that you bring with you onto your training and the buttons that can get pushed as a response to that.

This ongoing dynamic in regards to the development of his identity as a clinical psychologist post-qualification is something which LG is mindful of and reflects on often. However, to a large extent, LG has learned to embrace and accept this feeling of difference from other psychologists as part of his professional identity, mirroring the sense of acceptance seen more generally:

DH: I think initially you might have felt like you needed to conform to being a certain way, so this belief about I don't fit in and I must fit in, I don't think that's so strong now, I think there's a sense of I'm actually OK with who I am, my sense is that, you feel more confident about what you've got to offer. . . .

DH: I think there's a slight tongue in cheek when you talk about being different, I think that's good and I think you actually value that now.

The conversation also touched on the integration of a trainee's background into this professional identity:

DH: Your professional identity really linked to your personal views about yourself and identity, and that sense of going the extra mile, you know, some of the frustrations that I had for you were around your time management and looking after yourself and that sense of sort of . . . needing to be valued is what came up for me and, and being helpful, and how those drivers again really impacted on your identity.

LG: I can't escape my own background, I've kind of reflected on this, working class background, that idea of hard work and *first one in, last one out* mentality being quite a strong narrative in my family.

This also highlighted a potential risk if those attributes are not identified and reflected on with regards to the wider political and organisational context, especially in regards to his own values of needing to go that extra mile:

LG: And actually it can be quite a dangerous to have in an organisation under threat, and I think I've said a couple of times, the NHS will always take extra from you . . . there's always more to do.

Reflecting on this theme, the background, personal experiences and values of a person will undoubtedly influence his/her career choices and the development of his/her individual professional identity, as these factors are drawn together alongside the experience of clinical training. It is important, therefore, that supervision represents a safe space in which these elements can be identified and discussed openly and safely. If this can be achieved without it being perceived as a threat to a person's sense of self, supervision can act as a catalyst for ongoing professional development, while also helping us to be mindful of the experiences in our lives which may also have a detrimental impact on the clinical psychologists we aspire to be.

Theme four: 'evaluation and modelling against others'

One theme which emerged was the role of evaluation against others, and developing professional models based on the identity of others. This was noted as something which emerged as a characteristic during supervision on placement:

DH: A lot of evaluating yourself against your peers, and also the expectations of how you thought I as your supervisor viewed you. . . .
LG: you can't escape that on the course because, you are constantly evaluated, you are constantly aware that you as my supervisor ultimately hold the pass/ fail decision of my placement.

LG identified that not only was there an ongoing sense of comparison to trainee peers, which may be expected given the intensity and competition of doctoral training, but also a more complex dynamic between supervisor and supervisee. LG reflected on the roles that supervisors throughout his career have held in shaping his professional identity:

LG: I've always considered the way that my professional identity was shaped, was through the supervisors I've had, I've really modelled part of them I've liked and took, and tried to take attributes of theirs that really fit with my values and the person that I want to be, and the professional that I want to be.

While this reflects previously discussed difficulties in establishing what a good psychologist should look like, this also brings into consideration an interesting relationship dynamic between trainee and supervisors on clinical placement. The trainee is attempting to learn from and integrate aspects of his/her supervisor into his/her own professional identity, while also being acutely aware of the power afforded to said supervisor over him/her as part of placement; throughout clinical psychology training, clinical supervisors are responsible for evaluating a trainee's competencies and ultimately determine whether they pass their placement. While LG and DH were able to name and explore this difficult dynamic as part of supervision, if this does not feel safe to do, then there may be an impact on identity development with the trainee potentially adopting a superficial *mirror* of the supervisor in order to please him/her enough to pass the placement.

The conversation also explored this sense of comparison and its impact on ongoing sense of professional development following qualification. LG was the only newly qualified psychologist in the locality, and the few psychologists that were immediately available to him were in more senior positions, primarily on a part-time basis (some had been previous supervisors on other placements). Reflecting on this, having these individuals as the most available professional models from which to continue building a post-qualification professional identity is likely to have had an impact, given the comparative difference between them:

DH: There were times when you were really comparing yourself to your qualified peers, around where they were and the expectations of where you thought you should be, so again that kind of, self-evaluation, other to self stuff that was coming in. . . .

LG: how hard I was on myself in retrospect, comparing myself to peers who had been in positions for five, six or seven years, and actually, this was my first post, there were fewer psychologists on the ground so I don't have that many models as to what, what, what a psychologist should look like in this organisation.

This led to a sense of professional loneliness and isolation as a psychologist, and a strengthening of that sense of comparison and evaluation in relation to more senior or highly-banded peers outside of it:

LG: Actually I was a newly qualified psychologist in an organisation of my peers, and in this building, who are all 8as and 8bs[1] above me and, and it's quite a lonely position at times. . . .

LG: just thinking there for a moment, what would it have been like if we still had a psychology team, and I'm thinking of some of my colleagues and ex-trainees who, work in offices surrounded by psychologists and, actually my role is, I sit, on my own, for the first year at least, in a room of other professionals who aren't psychologists. . . .

DH: I look at a lot of those people now who are 8b psychologists in the organisation and they'll all be clear about their reasons for coming back to work here . . . because we had a really strong psychology team . . . maybe its partly about time or maybe something about they had a real sense of grounding about what it was to be a psychologist within a mental health setting.

The transition from a training to qualified position in this environment involved a significant shift. LG had a strong sense of professional identity as a trainee clinical psychologist, surrounded by peers of a similar level of skill/experience and educators/supervisors who acted as potential role models, continuing to strengthen and form this sense of identity. This professional identity shifted to one in which those points of contact were less evident, and the surrounding non-psychology professionals had their own discipline-specific sense of identity. The difference in pay scale bandings (related to levels of responsibility and job role) between psychologists was identified as a factor here; these differences can influence relationships to a large extent within the established hierarchy of the NHS.

One way of understanding the potential wider impact of this theme is through the notion of *communities of practice* (Lave & Wenger, 1991, 1998). This term refers to groups of people who share a particular interest or profession, and through the process of sharing information and experiences develop both personally and professionally. There is great value in learning alongside other developing psychologists, and the existence of an established or coherent group who can share the informal learning and experience of what it is to be a professional psychologist with a newer member of the profession can be useful in helping shape the development of a professional identity.

Theme five: 'interpersonal and intrapersonal influences – the impact on the supervisor'

A theme which permeated most others but also stood on its own was the interpersonal (relationship between supervisor/supervisee) and intrapersonal (personal thoughts, beliefs, attitudes and reflections) factors that are an integral part of supervision (Greben & Ruskin, 1994). This conversation highlighted the impact of this on the supervisor.

DH: I think it was quite a chunk of time, where the stuffing was knocked out of you, it was quite heart-breaking to see, you know, in terms of that, and a sense of almost, for me, a sense of powerlessness to act and it got me into an interesting place around my own reflections as your supervisor. . . . on the one hand holding this idea that I can be a good role model and on the other oh god I'm not good enough, you know, I'm not where he would aspire to be, you know, so that's been kind of interesting as well, so my own self-evaluation in terms of our work together.

When considering the developmental aspects of supervision with an underlying assumption of ongoing growth there would be an expectation of a change in dynamics as the supervisee gains experience (Worthington, 1987):

DH: Out of everyone I've worked with in terms of that preceptorship you've been the most explicit, so early on, about where you think you should be, I think that's been different, so whether that's pulled something in me . . . and whether that's linked to your own expectations of yourself, not that they are unrealistic expectations, but whether its, it's a sort of sense of, wow, he's already thinking about that and he hasn't even got to this bit yet, so that's interesting.

On further reflection, DH wondered whether this specific aspect was also linked to gender identity, which in this context may be specifically relevant for a male in a female dominated profession (80% female to 20% male; Farndon, 2016). LG alluded to during the conversation:

LG: Potentially what's expected of me and if we think about my gender and all the stuff there, the expectation that I would eventually enter a more senior role or a leadership position.

There may be an implicit, self-imposed pressure from such an expectation which has meant that issues around professional development have been much more at the forefront in this relationship. Looking at the experiences for men in such settings, Simpson (2004) highlighted three factors: men benefit from their minority status through assumptions of enhanced leadership (the assumed authority effect), by being given differential treatment (the special consideration effect) and being associated with a more careerist attitude to work (the career effect). Discussion of these factors is beyond the remit of this chapter, but these influences are likely to be impacting on professional sense of self, even at this early stage of LG's career.

Conclusion

The development of a professional identity in clinical psychology is characterised as a complex process involving the interaction of a wide range of internal and external factors, only a handful of which have been able to be identified and briefly examined here. This chapter highlights the importance of the supervisory relationship in encouraging reflection, reflexivity and creating a space in which it feels safe to explore these complex, both during and following the completion of training.

What has become most apparent though through this discussion was the need to more explicitly consider and account for the impact of the wider systems and organisational/political landscapes as a major contributing factor in development of identity, as the wider NHS continues to undertake ongoing and far-reaching change. If psychology as a profession is too thin on the ground, if psychologists become too caught up in the day-to-day battles of fire-fighting and holding a splintered system together or if senior clinicians are unable to act as effective role models to the next generation of clinicians, then this will have a significant impact on a trainee's development of professional identity. However, this may also mean that as a profession we need to adapt to these ongoing threats to maintain this professional development, considering our role within the healthcare system, better utilising existing professional structures, or developing newer methods or organisations with a shared purpose (e.g., with professionals on social media) to try and enact change or link together.

We need to embrace professional leadership as a core element of our professional identity to try and move organisations to healthier positions, all while supporting staff engagement and wellbeing. This will require strong leadership from clinical psychologists, not only at a local, service-based level. However it will also ensure that we are able to better influence the wider organisational and political structures that surround us.

Note

1 Referring to NHS Agenda for Change pay bands. At the time of writing, trainee clinical pscyhologists are employed on NHS Band 6; newly qualified clinical psychologists are generally employed at NHS Band 7. See www.nhsemployers.org/your-workforce/pay-and-reward/agenda-for-change/pay-scales/annual for more details.

Suggested further reading

Clance, P. R., & Imes, S. A. (1978). The imposter phenomenon in high achieving women: Dynamics and therapeutic intervention. *Psychotherapy: Theory, Research & Practice, 15*(3), 241–247.

O'Donovan, A., Halford, W. K., & Walters, B. (2011). Towards best practice supervision of clinical psychology trainees. *Australian Psychologist, 46*, 101–112.

Stokoe, P. (2011). *The healthy and the unhealthy organization: How can we help teams to remain effective?* In A. Rubitel & D. Reiss (Eds.), *Containment in the community: Supportive frameworks for thinking about antisocial behaviour and mental health* (pp. 237–259). London: Karnac/The Portman Papers.

References

Braun, V., & Clarke, V. (2006). Using thematic analysis in psychology. *Qualitative Research in Psychology, 3*(2), 77–101. doi:10.1191/1478088706qp063oa

British Psychological Society. (2014). *DCP policy on supervision*. Leicester: British Psychological Society.

Clance, P. R., & Imes, S. A. (1978). The imposter phenomenon in high achieving women: Dynamics and therapeutic intervention. *Psychotherapy: Theory, Research and Practice, 15*(3), 241–247. doi:10.1037/h0086006

Elman, N. S., Illfelder-Kaye, J., & Robiner, W. N. (2005). Professional development: Training for professionalism as a foundation for competent practice in psychology. *Professional Psychology: Research and Practice, 36*(4), 367–375. doi:10.1037/0735-7028.36.4.367

Farndon, H. (2016). *HCPC registered psychologists in the UK*. Leicester: British Psychological Society.

Gilbert, P. (2009). *The compassionate mind*. London: Constable & Robinson.

Gilburt, H. (2018). *Funding and staffing of NHS mental health providers: Still waiting for parity*. London: The King's Fund.

Greben, S. E., & Ruskin, R. (1994). *Clinical perspectives on psychotherapy supervision*. Arlington, VA: American Psychiatric Association.

Lave, J., & Wenger, E. (1991). *Situated learning: Legitimate peripheral participation*. Cambridge, UK: Cambridge University Press.

Lave, J., & Wenger, E. (1998). *Communities of practice: Learning, meaning, and identity*. Cambridge, UK: Cambridge University Press.

O'Donovan, A., Halford, W. K., & Walters, B. (2011). Towards best practice supervision of clinical psychology trainees. *Australian Psychologist, 46*, 101–112. doi:10.1111/j.1742-9544.2011.00033.x

Simpson, R. (2004). Masculinity at work: The experiences of men in female dominated occupations. *Work, Employment and Society, 18*(2), 349–368. doi:10.1177/0950017 2004042773

Stokoe, P. (2011). *The healthy and the unhealthy organization: How can we help teams to remain effective?* In A. Rubitel & D. Reiss (Eds.), *Containment in the community: Supportive frameworks for thinking about antisocial behaviour and mental health* (pp. 237–259). London: Karnac/The Portman Papers.

Worthington, E. L. (1987). Changes in supervision as counselors and supervisors gain experience: A review. *Professional Psychology, 18*, 189–208. doi:10.1037/0735-7028. 18.3.189

Chapter 14

Professional and personal identities as clinical psychologists

Being human

Hayley Higson and Sophie Allan

Summary points

- The concept of identity is a significant consideration among those progressing throughout a career in clinical psychology. While professional identity remains important, so too do the additional identities held by trainees.
- Dual identity, referring to those who identify as a psychologist and someone with lived experience of mental distress, brings an added layer of complexity, particularly when considering how to disclose this in educational and work contexts.
- External challenges can impact on trainees' wellbeing and, as such, the importance of taking time out for self-care ought to be advocated and encouraged. Supervision is one method whereby this may be explored further.

The concept of identity

Identity has been the object of discussion across a number of disciplines including sociology, philosophy and psychology. In the psychological literature it has been defined in terms of self-concept, self-awareness and self-efficacy, among others (Leary & Tangney, 2014). Gergen's (1971) theory presents self-concept as consisting multiple identities which each contain its own knowledge. Oyserman, Elmore, and Smith (2014) remark that identities are not static but "dynamically constructed in the moment" (p. 70).

Tajfel and Turner's *social identity theory* (1979) defined identity in terms of in/out group membership. They proposed that identity is determined by the groups within which we regard ourselves as members, and our relationships with these groups are suggested to be influential in relation to our wellbeing. Occupation is one specific group which may form part of identity, and *professional identity* is a distinct concept within this (Schein, 1978). Each of these theories can be considered in relation to a clinical psychology career path.

Specific identities held by aspiring and qualified psychologists

Aspiring, trainee and qualified clinical psychologists have dynamic personal identities just as anyone else – defining themselves as a friend, son/daughter, sibling, partner, parent and so on. Through the process of becoming a clinical psychologist, identities are being continually constructed and reconstructed as relationships, motivations and ideologies are reflected on and redefined. Clinical psychology training consists of a three-year postgraduate doctorate course, which involves a combination of clinical work, research and additional academic components. Therefore, as a trainee, one simultaneously becomes a student, NHS professional, researcher, supervisee and colleague. These shifting roles can change daily (e.g., professional on placement day, student during lectures), which can lead trainees to feel that their identity is fragmented. In reality, each of these identities has a dynamic relationship with each other which cannot be viewed in isolation; they change continuously as learning and experience develops.

Many trainees feel their identity should change immediately as a result of starting training or qualifying as a clinical psychologist. Entering clinical training is a significant milestone that has often involved many years of work and study: 58% of successful applicants to clinical psychology training in 2017 were aged 25–29 (Clearing House for Postgraduate Courses in Clinical Psychology, 2018). Being on a training programme represents membership of a new group (c.f. Tajfel & Turner, 1979). In reality, it can take time to adjust to these new roles which, while interesting and exciting, can also at times feel confusing or even disappointing.

Qualifying as a clinical psychologist brings the additional identities of senior clinician, supervisor and manager. This can be a significant departure from life as a trainee which is often relatively protected, for example with weekly supervision and often working with a smaller caseload of clients with less complex needs. While this is done in an attempt to support trainees to work within their level of competence and create a safe environment for learning, there can be benefits in exposing trainees to more levels of complexity and providing trainees with opportunities to voice opinions and practice their decision-making abilities. This may ease the transition from trainee to qualified clinical psychologist, which brings with it an increased level of responsibility and autonomy. This shift in role, and thus identity, often takes time to adjust to. Supervision at this point is vital. This is acknowledged by the British Psychological Society (BPS, 2014), who advocate that newly qualified psychologists should continue to receive hourly supervision on a weekly basis. In practice however, the demands of the NHS may mean that this is not always possible.

Dual identities

While it is important to consider professional identity within the milieu of the clinical psychology career pathway, it is also essential for other aspects of one's identity to be appreciated, particularly in relation to the interplay this may have with training. One such example is among those who recognise themselves to hold a *dual identity* as both a mental health professional and someone who has experienced their own mental health problems.

Clinical psychologists are no more immune to experiencing mental distress than the general population; indeed they may have an increased risk of depression and suicide (Charlemagne-Odle, Harmon, & Maltby, 2014). Low mood was experienced by 46% of psychological therapist respondents in a recent survey (BPS, 2016). Furthermore, in a survey exploring mental health amongst trainees, it was found that 67% reported having a lived experience of a mental health problem (Grice, Alcock, & Scior, 2018).

This goes against the commonly held assumption that clinical psychologists do not experience mental ill health. This has been termed the *them and us* myth in mental health work (Richards, 2010). Taking a *them and us* position can challenge a psychologist's sense of identity if he/she goes on to experience problems of his/her own, perhaps leading to a sense of fragmented identity rather than a coherent whole (Richards, Holttum, & Springham, 2016). In our experience, this can also present a challenge to personal values of authenticity when deciding whether or not to disclose personal experiences to colleagues, peers and supervisors. Recent campaigns such as *Only Us* (https://twitter.com/OnlyUsCampaign) and *in2gr8 mental health* (www.in2gr8mentalhealth.com) have sought to challenge this dynamic, and encourage and support people to be more open about their mental health difficulties. However, this is not without challenge.

Having a dual identity affects training and work in both positive and negative ways. Lived experience may result in more authentic empathy in the therapeutic relationship, greater perspective or life experience, and a sign of increased resilience. Conversely there is the possibility of over identification with clients who may have experienced similar difficulties, teaching on related topics to the person's own experience may also be distressing, and arguably there is increased vulnerability to the stresses associated with the career path. Of course this depends on the individual and where he/she is in relation to his/her mental health difficulties.

In order to manage a dual identity as a trainee clinical psychologist, we would suggest that the person firstly needs to acknowledge this aspect of his/her identity. This can often be a challenge, as confusion may exist about whether one is experiencing a mental health difficulty that is serious enough to warrant that label; for example, it can be difficult to know whether one is experiencing heightened levels of anxiety in acute response to current stress, or whether one is feeling low in mood because of recent events in one's life. Similarly, retaining the sense of dual identity when one feels one is mentally healthy or have recovered may ignite worries about inappropriately adopting this identity. This is where peer support can be invaluable.

Seeking support (either face to face or online) from peers who also have a dual identity or are sympathetic to the issues, and identifying role models who are open about their lived experience, can be vital in allowing people the space to reflect on their dual identity and consider its place within the working context. Accessing such support does however rely on people speaking up to share their stories. In our experience, it is important to acknowledge our own vulnerabilities and anticipate times when self-care may be particularly important, for example being prepared to take extra breaks in lecture topics which may be personally relevant, and seeking support from supervisors and peers where clinical cases resonate with our own experiences.

Within the workplace specifically, the presence of stigma can create a culture of silence, which stifles the ability to harness transparency amongst health professionals about their own mental health needs (Moll, 2014). While disclosing personal vulnerabilities can be challenging and require forethought, facilitating dialogues on psychological wellbeing is viewed as an overall positive move in tackling stigma. This choice of whether or not to disclose these difficulties is a personal one that should be given space for reflection.

In a review of the available literature on the decision to share experiences of mental health problems in the workplace, Brohan, Henderson and Wheat (2012) found that there are a number of factors which affect an employee's decision of whether or not to share details regarding his/her mental health. Reasons behind the decision to disclose were found to be influenced by the needs for adjustments and support in the work place, previous positive experiences of disclosure, a need to be honest and act as role models for others and as a result of the stress caused by attempts to conceal mental health difficulties. Alternatively, the factors which contributed to the decision of not disclosing were as a result of assumptions that others lack interest, the rights to privacy and aims to conceal part of a perceived stigmatised identity.

In the UK specifically, stigma and negative attitudes remain around mental health problems, despite campaigns aimed at reducing these negative attitudes (Dean & Phillips, 2015). Stigma continues to inform peoples' choice to disclose mental health needs which may impact on the help-seeking behaviour of trainees who connect with dual identity. Disclosing vulnerabilities can also present a challenge in the supervisor-supervisee relationship during clinical psychology training, where the supervisor is required to make judgements about the trainee's competence and whether he/she passes the placement, thus holding a position of power.

Impact of external challenges on identities

Whether or not a person considers him/herself to hold a dual identity of this sort, it is important to recognise that a doctorate in clinical psychology is indeed a challenging and stressful programme for a variety of reasons (Cushway, 1992; Pica, 1998). Experiences of imposter syndrome (Clance & Imes, 1978), performance anxiety, ambiguity and unmet expectations (Skovholt & Rønnestad, 2003) all serve to magnify the challenges. Not least, the constant exposure to deadlines and assessment of both clinical and academic components of the work create added pressures (Kleespies, 1993), especially as trainees are expected to manage ongoing competing demands.

While the course is demanding in its own right, trainees bring with them diverse identities and personal contexts which may generate external challenges which further impact upon their wellbeing. Life does not stop merely because one embarks upon the clinical psychology doctorate. Challenges such as experiencing bereavement, physical health problems, relationship difficulties, financial problems and injuries can touch the lives of people whilst they are training. Worryingly, Spiegelman and Werth (2005) reported that when affected by bereavement, trainees often feel that they do not have the necessary space to process the bereavement reaction as a result of the demands of training.

The practicalities of meeting the multiple, and potentially conflicting, needs of trainees, services (including their service users) and courses can be challenging to navigate. While a trainee may be unable to work with people who have stories which resonate with his/her own, there may be specific difficulties in establishing this before meeting with that person. Occasionally, referrals and indeed case notes may omit important information that is only identified when a service user engages in an assessment. This may create difficulties for both the trainee and service user. While the trainee may encounter a shift in focus and emotional state, the service user may feel unheard and overlooked. This could negatively shape his/her perceptions of services and ultimately influence further engagement. After a difficult session, trainees who would benefit from de-briefing with supervisors or peers may find this difficult to achieve, either due to a lack of staff availability or from being based in isolated clinics away from an office base.

It is therefore imperative for trainees and training courses to acknowledge the multiple identities held by many people pursuing a career in clinical psychology, and to be aware of the contextual demands that may create additional challenges. Cushway (1992) found that the multiple demands of training can result in trainees finding it difficult to engage in practices of self-care. As a result, courses could begin to harness dialogues on the importance of self-care and help-seeking throughout training and beyond, for instance by giving specific lectures on the topic. Indeed the BPS (2001) advocates the practice of self-care due to its influence on professional work, and as such this message should be disseminated widely to ensure that self-care is prioritised. This would benefit trainees post qualification and could promote a compassionate approach that grants trainees with *permission* to engage in self-care.

Direct supervision could be one process whereby context and engagement with self-care is explored, yet there is also a need for role models who engage with self-care within the work environment, for example by demonstrating clear boundary setting through taking regular breaks and not working outside of contracted hours. While this may be a challenge in the current climate, it should be a priority given the increasing pressures on mental health professionals and the associated rates of staff sickness (Hacker-Hughes et al., 2016).

Role of supervision and reflection

Supervisors are often in a position of power and influence, so while trainees are often encouraged to be open and honest throughout training, the disclosure of difficulties may be particularly difficult due to the evaluative nature of the course, and the role supervisors have within this process.

Inskipp and Proctor's (2001) model of clinical supervision comprises of three elements: *formative, normative* and *restorative*. It is advocated that supervision touches on each element as needs arise. *Normative* refers to addressing the managerial requirements of the role whereas *formative* involves the process of using supervision for skill and knowledge development. The *restorative* component reflects the supportive nature of supervision and the importance for supervisors and supervisee to consider the role of external challenges, and the impact that these may have upon clinical work. Such discussions may be particularly beneficial for trainees to reflect on their own vulnerabilities and to evaluate their own means of managing stresses.

Alternative models of supervision also include details on the importance of dedicating time to consider the external demands on the supervisee. Hawkins & Shohet (1989) highlight the importance of context, and Rønnestad and Skovolt's (1993) model explicitly considers the influences of personal life on supervision and professional development.

However, the restorative elements of supervision can be overlooked when clinical work and a thirst for more knowledge takes priority. It therefore seems imperative that this restorative component is routinely addressed in the supervisory context, perhaps as the first item on a supervision agenda. If this is achieved, supervision has the ability to provide a valuable resource, enabling trainees to enhance self-awareness and coping strategies. This can provide trainees with a strong foundation upon which to build as a qualified clinical psychologist. However challenges to this include the extent to which the supervisee feels able to trust his/her supervisor with personal information, and whether there is another time for these discussions after other topics (such as clinical cases) are discussed.

A trainee's right to privacy should also be respected, yet simultaneously an understanding of the value of exploring the restorative elements of supervision needs to be approached. In particular, trainees should be made aware of the influence of external stresses and situations upon clinical work. Supervisory contracts, agenda setting and discussions of the multiple features of clinical supervision at initial meetings may therefore allow supervisors and supervisees to collaboratively agree on when and how restorative elements of supervision will be addressed.

Conclusion

Within this chapter we have discussed the intricate nature of professional identity for those on a clinical psychology career pathway. There are additional challenges which trainees may encounter as a result of holding dual identities and their experience of additional challenges outside of the course. The role of supervision, and the importance of utilising restorative practise within supervision, is vital in allowing trainees to develop their self-awareness and, with that, acceptance of their own vulnerability.

Suggested further reading

Harris, R. (2008). *The happiness trap*. London: Constable & Robinson Ltd.

Hughes, J., & Youngson, S. (2009). *Personal development and clinical psychology*. Sussex: John Wiley & Sons Ltd.

Kolts, R. L., Bell, T., Bennett-Levy, J., & Irons, C. (2018). *Experiencing compassion-focused therapy from the inside out: A self-practice/self-reflection workbook for therapists*. London: Guilford Press.

Wicks, R. J. (2007). *The resilient clinician*. New York, NY: Oxford University Press.

References

British Psychological Society. (2001). *Professional practice guidelines: Division of clinical psychology*. Retrieved from www.bps.org.uk/sites/default/files/documents/professional_practice_guidelines_-_division_of_clinical_psychology.pdf

British Psychological Society. (2014). *DCP policy on supervision*. Retrieved from https://www1.bps.org.uk/system/files/Public%20files/inf224_dcp_supervision.pdf

BritishPsychologicalSociety.(2016).*Promotingthewell-beingofmentalhealthprofessionals*. Retrievedfromwww.bps.org.uk/news/promoting-wellbeing-mental-health-professionals

Brohan, E., Henderson, C., & Wheat, K. (2012). Systematic review of beliefs, behaviours and influencing factors associated with disclosure of a mental health problem in the workplace. *BMC Psychiatry, 12*, 11. doi:10.1186/1471-244X-12-11

Charlemagne-Odle, S., Harmon, G., & Maltby, M. (2014). Clinical psychologists' experiences of personal significant distress. *Psychology and Psychotherapy: Theory, Research and Practice, 87*(2), 237–252. doi:10.1111/j.2044-8341.2012.02070.x

Clance, P. R., & Imes, S. A. (1978). The imposter phenomenon in high achieving women: Dynamics and therapeutic intervention. *Psychotherapy: Theory, Research & Practice, 15*(3), 241–247. doi:10.1037/h0086006

Clearing House for Postgraduate Courses in Clinical Psychology. (2018). *Equal opportunities: 2017 entry*. Retrieved from www.leeds.ac.uk/chpccp/equalopps2017.html

Cushway, D. (1992). Stress in clinical psychology trainees. *British Journal of Clinical Psychology, 31*(2), 169–179. doi:10.1111/j.2044-8260.1992.tb00981.x

Dean, L., & Phillips, M. (2015). *British social attitudes: Attitudes to mental health problems and mental wellbeing*. London: Public Health England. Retrieved from www.bsa.natcen.ac.uk/media/39109/phe-bsa-2015-attitudes-to-mental-health.pdf

Gergen, K. J. (1971). *The concept of self*. New York, NY: Holt, Rinehart & Winston.

Grice, T., Alcock, K., & Scior, K. (2018). Mental health disclosure among clinical psychologists in training: Perfectionism and pragmatism. *Clinical Psychology and Psychotherapy*. doi:10.1002/cpp.2192

Hacker-Hughes, J., Rao, A. S., Dosanjh, N., Cohen-Tovée, E., Clarke, J., & Bhutani, G. (2016). Physician heal thyself (Luke 4:23). *British Journal of Psychiatry, 209*, 447–448. doi:10.1192/bjp.bp.116.185355

Hawkins, P., & Shohet, R. (1989). *Supervision in the helping professions: An individual, group, and organizational approach*. Milton Keynes, UK: Open University Press.

Inskipp, F., & Proctor, B. (2001). *Making the most of supervision: Part 1*. Twickenham: Cascade.

Kleespies, P. M. (1993). The stress of patient suicidal behaviour: Implications for interns and training programs in psychology. *Professional Psychology: Research and Practice*, *24*, 477–482. doi:10.1037/0735-7028.24.4.477

Leary, M. R., & Tangney, J. P. (Eds.). (2014). *Handbook of self and identity* (2nd ed.). New York, NY: Guilford Press.

Moll, S. E. (2014). The web of silence: A qualitative case study of early intervention and support for healthcare workers with mental ill-health. *BMC Public Health*, *14*, 138. doi:10.1186/1471-2458-14-138

Oyserman, D., Elmore, K., & Smith, G. (2014). Self, self-concept and identity. In M. R. Leary & J. P. Tangey (Eds.), *Handbook of self and identity* (pp. 69–104). New York, NY: Guilford Press.

Pica, M. (1998). The ambiguous nature of clinical training and its impact on the development of student clinicians. *Psychotherapy: Theory, Research, Practice, Training*, *35*(3), 361–365. doi:10.1037/h0087840

Richards, C. (2010). "Them and us" in mental health services. *The Psychologist*, *23*(1), 40–41.

Richards, J., Holttum, S., & Springham, N. (2016). How do mental health professionals who are also or have been mental health service users construct their identities? *SAGE Open*, 1–14. doi:10.1177/2158244015621348

Rønnestad, M. H., & Skovholt, T. M. (1993). Supervision of beginning and advanced graduate students of counselling and psychotherapy. *Journal of Counselling and Development*, *71*, 396–405. doi:10.1002/j.1556-6676.1993.tb02655.x

Schein, E. H. (1978). *Career dynamics: Matching individual and organizational needs*. Reading, MA: Addison-Wesley.

Skovholt, T. M., & Rønnestad, M. H. (2003). Struggles of the novice counsellor and therapist. *Journal of Career Development*, *30*, 45–58. Retrieved from www.sv.uio.no/psi/personer/vit/emeritus/helgero/StrugglesJCD.pdf

Spiegelman, J. S., & Werth, J. L., Jr. (2005). Don't forget about me: The experiences of therapists-in-training after a client has attempted or died by suicide. In K. M. Weiner (Ed.), *Therapeutic and legal issues for therapists who have survived a client suicide: Breaking the silence* (pp. 35–57). New York, NY: Haworth Press.

Tajfel, H., & Turner, J. C. (1979). An integrative theory of intergroup conflict. In W. D. Austin & S. Worchel (Eds.), *The social psychology of intergroup relations* (pp. 33–47). Monterey, CA: Brooks/Cole.

Glossary of terms

Acceptance and commitment therapy (ACT) A 'third-wave' behavioural therapy developed in the 1980s focusing on acceptance of unwanted difficulties and committed values–driven action, rather than behavioural change (see Harris, 2006, for an overview of ACT).

Austerity Government fiscal policy in this context introduced by the Conservative Government in England in 2008/2009. In short, austerity measures aim to reduce public spending to tackle budget deficits and national debt. These measures coincided with the beginning of changes to the welfare system.

CAMHS Child and adolescent mental health services (CAMHS) support children and young people experiencing difficulties with their physical, behavioural and psychological wellbeing.

Clinical supervision A process which has the specific purpose to maintain, update and develop clinical skills in assessment, formulation and interventions; the function is to ensure safe and effective practice within a respectful and trusting relationship.

Cognitive-behavioural therapy A talking therapy that can help people to manage their psychological difficulties by changing the way they think and behave.

Collaboration The mutual involvement of client and therapist in a helping relationship.

Community psychology The study of individuals' contexts within *communities* and the wider society, and the relationships of the individual to *communities* and society. *Community psychologists* seek to understand the quality of life of individuals within groups, organisations and institutions, *communities* and society.

Context (in relation to an individual) Considering a person's context means looking at the impact their culture, community, society, family, government and other systems have on them as an individual.

Disability Living Allowance and Personal Independence Payment These are what might be considered 'disability benefits'. DLA is being gradually replaced by PIP. These benefits are designed to support a person to meet any additional costs they might incur in life because of their disability, to enable them to live as independently as possible.

Emergent awareness   The emergence of a verbal acknowledgment of deficits as a consequence of the person attempting to act on them and recognising their errors or mistakes.

Executive functioning   'Higher order' cognitive functions most commonly associated with the frontal areas of the brain, including the ability to problem solve, switch attention and control impulses.

Fitness to work assessments   To claim some benefits, a person must attend an assessment to determine whether he/she is able to work, despite claiming to have a disability.

Formulation   A psychological formulation is a way of understanding the factors underlying distress in such a way that it informs the changes that may help reduce that distress and the mechanisms by which such change may occur.

Government policy   Sets out the government's expectations and intentions about certain topics (for example drugs, mental health), usually aimed to bring about change in those areas.

Health and Care Professions Council   This is the government body that regulates some psychologists, including clinical psychologists, and other professions working in health and care settings in England. The HCPC sets standards that must be followed and investigates professionals who have fallen short of those standards.

Human rights–based approach   Putting human rights and human rights principles at the heart of policy and planning, empowering staff and service users with the knowledge, skills and the organisational leadership and commitment to achieve human rights–based approaches.

Improving Access to Psychological Therapies (IAPT)   A government programme designed to expand the availability of psychological therapies across the UK. Initially designed for adults, IAPT is now available for young people, and for those with long-term health conditions. IAPT services typically offer interventions based on cognitive-behaviour therapy, usually provided by psychological wellbeing practitioners (PWPs) and cognitive-behavioural therapists.

Institutional racism   Racism is often thought to refer to people being personally racist – for example, engaging in overtly and explicitly racist verbal abuse or actively treating people differently because of their ethnicity. However, a series of government inquiries have identified that, within institutions such as the police or health service, people from black and other minority ethnic backgrounds can be treated differently – usually worse – even if individual members of those institutions do not individually act in this way; the institutions themselves operate in discriminatory ways through entrenched attitudes and norms.

Integrative   The combining of two or more approaches to form a holistic understanding.

Inter-disciplinary   Involving two or more professional disciplines (i.e., clinical psychology, psychiatry, occupation therapy etc.).

Marginalisation   Social exclusion or marginalisation refers to social disadvantage and relegation to the fringes of society, often accompanied by 'drowning out' of the marginalised person's views. People are often marginalised when their characteristics – such as their gender, sexuality, race or their class – are considered to be 'undesirable'.

Motivational interviewing   A collaborative approach for working with ambivalence to behavioural change using motivational techniques, developed by Miller and Rollnick (1991, 2002).

Neuropsychological   Relating to the relationship between the brain and a persons' behaviour, emotion and cognition.

Person-centred approach   This is an approach to service provision which ensures that the people who use health and social care services are seen as equal partners in the decisions around their care. This approach advocates supporting people to live an enriched and independent life, guided by the principles of dignity, respect and compassion and tailored around a person's needs and individual strengths.

Person-centred therapy   An approach which places the client as the expert in him/herself, trusting him/her to reach his/her full potential through the support of a therapeutic relationship that provides understanding acceptance and genuineness, developed from the work of the psychologist Dr Carl Rogers (1902–1987).

Power dynamics   The way different people or groups of people interact with each other and one of these sides is more powerful than the other.

Professional identity   The way in which we see ourselves as professional practitioners; the way in which we present ourselves professionally to others and the way in which others perceive us as professionals.

Public health   Aims to increase awareness about health issues, attempting to prevent illness and disease by researching and educating society about health issues. For example there are a number of public health campaigns to inform people about the adverse affects of smoking, designed to change the behaviours of people who smoke (to stop them smoking).

Reflective practice   Reflective practice is understood as the process of learning through and from experience towards gaining new insights of self and/ or practice.

Relational patterns   An individual's patterns of relating to others and him/ herself, formed over time through experiences of interpersonal interactions.

Risk assessment   The collection of information to determine the likelihood of harm occurring.

Risk management   The implementation of a set of strategies or ideas aimed at reducing the likelihood of risk occurring.

Social justice   A political and philosophical concept which holds that all people should have equal access to wealth, health, wellbeing, *justice* and opportunity.

It rejects the notion that certain characteristics should automatically place you in a position of privilege over others who lack those characteristics.

Stages of change model　A five-stage model (precontemplation, contemplation, preparation, action and maintenance) of an individual's readiness to change a particular problematic behaviour, developed by Prochaska and DiClemente (1982).

Supervision　Supervision is a space where psychologists can reflect on their day-to-day work, usually with someone more experienced, in order to positively impact their practice.

Systemic　These approaches consider the individual within their system, rather than only as individuals. Systemic thinking promotes the idea that we exist in systems – families, communities and societies – and that our difficulties lie in the interactions between different parts of that system. Consequently, for any meaningful change to occur, all parts of the system must change.

Therapeutic Alliance/Relationship　The relationship between a psychologist or therapist and the client, which allows them to work together to bring about change in therapy.

Therapeutic Boundaries　Within the therapeutic alliance, there are certain boundaries in the relationship which make it different to relationships that happen outside of the therapy room. For example, therapy sessions are time limited, there are limits about what personal information a therapist might disclose to his/her client and the conversations in therapy are limited to what is relevant to working on the issues being worked on in therapy.

Uni-modal　Practicing within one model of therapy or within one psychological model or framework.

Welfare benefits and the welfare benefits systems　Refers to the system within the UK where individuals who cannot work, or have low income, can access welfare benefits (such as personal independence payment, employment support allowance, jobseeker's allowance) to support them to meet their needs.

Index

Milton Keynes UK
Ingram Content Group UK Ltd.
UKHW021854010923
427937UK00015B/120

9 781138 482982